Contents

Preface

This is a new edition of one of the most popular books in the SEB series. As in the previous edition and in his other books and column for the *Sunday Times*, David Smith writes with considerable authority and clarity.

This new edition examines the key features, and roles, of the microeconomic and macroeconomic policies of the government. It discusses how the government is seeking to achieve its objectives via greater stability in government policy, including the new relationship between the administration and the Bank of England, and the government's fiscal policy rules.

Susan Grant
Series Editor

STUDIES IN ECONOMICS AND BUSINESS

UK Current
Economic Policy

Third Edition

David Smith

Series Editor
Susan Grant
Abingdon and Witney College

Heinemann Educational Publishers
Halley Court, Jordan Hill, Oxford OX2 8EJ
Part of Harcourt Education

Heinemann is the registered trademark of
Harcourt Education Limited

First published in 1994 in the Studies in the UK Economy series
Second edition 1999
Third edition 2003

08 07 06 05 04 03
10 9 8 7 6 5 4 3 2 1

British Library Cataloguing in Publication Data is available
from the British Library on request.

ISBN 0 435 33228 7

Edited by Catherine Matthews
Typeset by Techtype, Abingdon, Oxon
Printed and bound in Great Britain by Biddles Ltd, *www.biddles.co.uk*

Original illustrations © Harcourt Education Limited, 2003

Illustrated by Techtype

Acknowledgements
Extracts
pp. 9, 14, 20, 27, 42, 54, 24, 81, 95, 106 Crown Copyright material is reproduced under
Class License Number C01W0000141 with the permission of the Controller of HMSO and
the Queen's Printer for Scotland. pp. 38, 51, 64, 78, 118 reproduced with the kind
permission of the OCR. pp. 29, *Brown's tax and spend* by Benedict Brogan; *The Brown
Bear* by G. Trefgarne 73; *Brown stalling on euro* by Toby Helm, 115 © Telegraph Group
Limited 2003. p. 34 *Tories prepare to defy leader in tartan tax* by David Scott © The
Scotsman Publications Limited. p. 46 © *City Gloom* by Larry Elliott and Charlotte Denny
© The Guardian. pp. 13, 51, 80, 117 are AQA examination questions reproduced by
permission of the Assessment and Qualifications Alliance. pp. 11, 39, 52, 78, 92 are Edexcel
examination questions reproduced by permission of London Qualifications Ltd.

Every effort has been made to contact copyright holders of material reproduced in this
book. Any omissions will be rectified in subsequent printings if notice is given to the
publishers.

Tel: 01865 888058 www.heinemann.co.uk

Introduction

This third edition of *UK Current Economic Policy* is actually the fifth edition in a sequence which began life as *Mrs Thatcher's Economics* in the 1980s; that book evolved into *Mrs Thatcher's Economics: Her Legacy*, which became the first and second editions of *UK Current Economic Policy*. Each book has been different from its predecessor, none more so than this one.

After 18 years in opposition, the Labour party took office in May 1997 determined to radically reform the economic policy process, most dramatically with the granting of operational independence – the power of setting interest rates – to the Bank of England. This change, within days of the general election, was but one of many. If you were to characterize the Labour government's approach it would be that, whereas in the past Labour chancellors of the exchequer soon found themselves bogged down in short-term economic management, and in particular sterling crises, this one was determined to minimize that risk, and concentrate on raising Britain's long-run economic performance and making a reality of its election slogan of offering 'equality of opportunity'.

The fact that economic policy has changed so much in the past 15–20 years is what makes the subject a fascinating one to study. Economics is a living subject. A few years ago, economists advised while politicians took the decisions. Now, with the Bank of England's monetary policy committee, we have a living example of economists taking decisions which influence everyday lives. Anybody who doubts whether economics is worth studying should bear this example in mind.

• About this book

In the following nine chapters, I describe the main areas of economic policy and the theory which lies behind them. In some cases there is room to provide only a brief introduction into a subject area, and I would urge students to read further, using the references at the end of each chapter, as well as the various websites listed. I would also, for obvious reasons, urge regular reading of the economics articles in newspapers and magazines, particularly, of course, my own contributions in the *Sunday Times* (www.sunday-times.co.uk). You can also read my other columns on my website (www.economicsuk.com).

Chapter 1 is about the role and limits of economic policy. It starts with the question: What is economic policy? It then touches on growth,

1

inflation and unemployment; the three ways of measuring gross domestic product; macroeconomic and microeconomic policy; aggregate demand and supply; objectives and instruments; and the modern response to the policy conflict.

Chapter 2 is about taxation: the tax burden; types of taxation; the principles of taxation; taxation, incentives and the supply side; the Laffer curve; tax cuts and the work/leisure trade-off; taxation and the distribution of income.

Chapter 3 covers public expenditure and the changing role of fiscal policy: fiscal policy; the modern welfare state; debts and deficits; deficits and 'crowding out'; the comprehensive spending review; the case for and against privatization; privatization and regulation; the National Asset Register.

Chapter 4 looks at the Bank of England and monetary policy. What is monetary policy and how does it work? It covers monetarism and the money supply; Bank of England independence (Is independence better?) and the inflation target; how Bank independence compares with other countries.

Chapter 5 is about employment. It covers the measurement of unemployment; traditional full employment (Whatever happened to it?); voluntary and involuntary unemployment; the unemployment/ inflation trade-off (the Phillips curve); the natural rate and the NAIRU; and modern 'full employment'.

Chapter 6 is about stability and economic growth: the business cycle; business-cycle theories; traditional counter-cyclical policies; Britain's cyclical experience; whether cyclical volatility reduces economic growth; and government policies for stability.

Chapter 7 looks at productivity and competition. What is productivity? Why does Britain lag behind? What policies can be used to boost productivity? Is there a trade-off between productivity and employment? Does competition boost productivity?

Chapter 8 examines devolution and regional policy: the regional problem; the rise and fall of regional policy; devolution; and the economics of independence.

Chapter 9 looks at Britain in Europe: the UK and the European Union; customs unions and common markets; European economic and monetary union; Britain, the ERM and 'Black Wednesday'; achieving EMU; the pros and cons of EMU; and Britain and the euro.

It may be that, by the time this book comes to be revised again, Britain will be part of the single currency and a further sea change will have occurred in UK economic policymaking. Until that happens, I hope this book will assist you, and I wish you every success.

Chapter One

The role and limits of economic policy

'It is the conquest of inflation, and not the pursuit of growth and employment, which is or should be the objective of macroeconomic *policy. And it is the creation of conditions conducive to growth and employment, and not the suppression of price rises, which is or should be the objective of* microeconomic *policy.'*
Nigel Lawson (as Chancellor of the Exchequer), Mais Lecture 1984

What is economic policy?

Most people would define economic policy as the core activities of a modern-day Chancellor of the Exchequer, together with those actions taken on behalf of the government by the Bank of England. Thus it includes decisions on:

- taxation – both the overall level and rates for individual taxes
- public expenditure – including the way it is divided between programmes, and between current and capital spending
- interest rates, and the growth of money and credit
- the external value of sterling, and whether it is fixed, floating, or intended to be part of the European single currency.

This, however, would be only a narrow definition of economic policy. When governments act to raise educational standards this has an effect, over the long term, on the nation's economic performance. A better educated workforce is usually a more productive one. The same is true for health. Investment in roads and the railways improves economic efficiency. Few actions of government do not affect the economy in some way.

No clear boundary exists at which economic policy stops and other policies begin. But it is necessary, in this book, to set some limits, specifically that of *defining economic policy as those actions by government whose intentions are mainly economic.*

Growth, inflation and unemployment

Let us begin with some basic definitions. When economists talk of economic growth, they mean the rate of growth of **gross domestic product** (GDP). This is measured in three ways. It is the sum total of all incomes and production in the economy, and all expenditures on goods produced in the economy. The totals should add up to the same overall figure, although in practice there is usually a significant statistical discrepancy. Table 1 shows the GDP, measured on the expenditure basis, for the UK in 2002.

Table 1 is useful because it sets out what is known as the 'national income identity'. GDP (sometimes called 'national income') is equal to private consumption plus government consumption plus investment plus any change in inventories (or stocks) plus exports, *less* imports. If we think of the two other ways of measuring GDP, income and production, we can see why this identity holds. Anything that is spent in Britain, together with anything that is spent by foreigners on British goods and services (exports), adds to British income and the value of British production. But anything that is produced abroad and sold here (imports) does not, and so has to be deducted to give our GDP figure.

Note that the table refers to GDP in 1995 prices. To measure the economy's growth rate, it is necessary to remove the inflation component from GDP. Otherwise periods of high inflation would wrongly appear to be periods of high growth. Adjusting for inflation in this way is known as 'deflating' GDP and the overall measure of inflation used to do this is called the **GDP deflator**.

The more common measure of inflation is, however, that which is measured by the **retail prices index**, or RPI. The government targets inflation according to a slightly different measure, the RPI excluding mortgage interest payments, or **RPIX**. The target for the latter is currently 2.5 per cent, although at some stage the government plans to switch to a new target based on the so-called harmonized index of

Table 1 2002 GDP (expenditure measure) at 1995 prices (£ billion)

Household consumption	608.8
General government consumption	163.8
Fixed investment	147.0
Change in inventories	0.6
Domestic demand (the sum of the above)	920.2
Exports, goods and services	283.8
Total final expenditure (all the above)	**1202.9**
Less imports, goods and services	342.6
Equals GDP at market prices	**860.3**

Source: Office for National Statistics

consumer prices (HICP), which uses the same method of calculation as other countries in Europe.

Two other important statistical variables are **unemployment** and the **balance of payments**. Unemployment has traditionally been measured by the claimant count – the number of people unemployed and claiming benefit. More recently the government has indicated that its preferred measure of unemployment is based on the Labour Force Survey, which includes people who are eligible for work but not entitled to benefit. In early 2003, unemployment was 0.9 million on the claimant count and 1.5 million on the LFS measure.

The balance of payments consists of two elements, the **current account** and the capital account. The two normally balance out: a country running a current account deficit – based on trade in goods and services plus other 'invisible' items of trade such as investment income from abroad and the City's earnings – requires a compensating inflow on the capital account.

Macroeconomic and microeconomic policy

Macroeconomic policy includes taxation and public spending, which together make up **fiscal policy**. Interest rates and the exchange rate are the key elements of **monetary policy**. Macroeconomic policy can also include *incomes policies*, which attempt to limit overall pay rises; *trade policy*, where Britain has favoured freeing international trade under the auspices of first the GATT (the General Agreement on Tariffs and Trade) and now the WTO (World Trade Organization); and *regional policy*, intended to influence the distribution of economic activity between regions.

Microeconomic policy consists of actions aimed at improving the economy's long-term growth potential, by acting on the **supply side**. Examples are:

- improving incentives for workers and entrepreneurs
- increasing and improving the supply of labour through government training schemes and welfare reform
- outlawing restrictive practices
- increasing competition
- ensuring that the financial system is an efficient supplier of finance for business expansion.

Modern microeconomic policy tries to raise economic efficiency by improving the workings of markets.

One way of characterizing the economic approach of the Labour government elected in May 1997 is that the Chancellor of the Exchequer, Gordon Brown, attempted to reduce the emphasis on day-to-day macroeconomic management, by granting operational independence to the Bank of England (control of interest rates) and by setting fiscal policy, both tax and public spending, in a medium-term context. That way, it was said, there could be a greater emphasis on microeconomic measures to improve long-run performance.

Macroeconomic policy, aggregate demand and aggregate supply

One common way of thinking about how macroeconomic policy operates is by means of **aggregate demand** and **aggregate supply**. An aggregate demand curve shows the overall level of demand in the economy for a series of price levels. As with a normal demand curve, the lower the price level the greater the demand. With an expansionary macroeconomic policy, for example, an increase in government spending has the effect of increasing aggregate demand at each price level. It pushes the aggregate demand curve outwards, from AD to AD_1 (see Figure 1).

To assess the overall impact of macroeconomic policy on the economy, it is necessary to introduce aggregate supply – the overall amount of goods and services supplied at each price level. Traditional **Keynesian** analysis assumed that, until full capacity in the economy was reached, governments could expand demand, and reduce unemployment, without increasing the price level. The assumption was

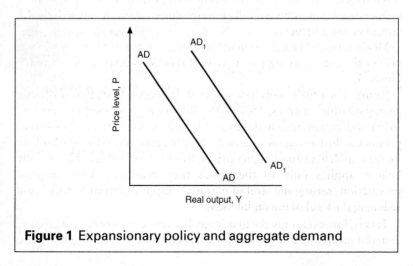

Figure 1 Expansionary policy and aggregate demand

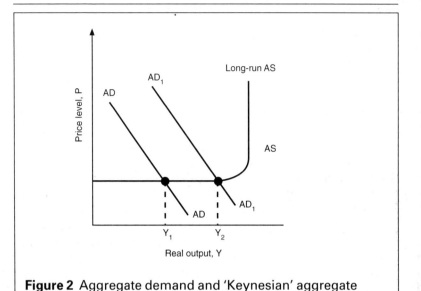

Figure 2 Aggregate demand and 'Keynesian' aggregate supply

of an aggregate supply curve which was horizontal until the point of full capacity (and full employment) was reached, whereupon it would become vertical – and further expansion of demand by the government would result only in higher prices. This is shown in Figure 2.

The shift in the aggregate demand curve from AD to AD_1 has the effect of pushing real output from Y_1 to Y_2, without affecting the price level. Thus, it seemed, governments should introduce expansionary policies until they achieved full employment – the point at which the AS curve becomes vertical.

Modern new classical (or **neoclassical**) economists, however, do not believe the aggregate supply curve is of this 'Keynesian' type. Examine Figure 3.

Figure 3 is a little more complicated. It shows, first, two *short-run* aggregate supply curves, AS and AS_1. When the government takes steps to expand aggregate demand from AD to AD_1, the initial response is to produce a shift along the aggregate supply curve AS. Firms see both an increase in demand and higher prices, from P_1 to P_2 (which they initially believe applies only to the goods they produce). They increase production, raising the level of national output (Y) from Y_1 to Y_2, and reducing the level of unemployment.

This is, however, only the first stage. Because the increase in aggregate demand pushes up not just the prices faced by individual firms but also

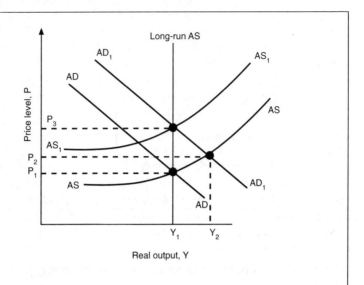

Figure 3 Aggregate demand and short-run and long-run aggregate supply

the general price level, the effect is to produce an increase in money wage rates (workers demand an increase in wages to compensate for higher prices). Once firms are faced with the need to pay higher money wages, the amount they are willing to supply at each price level falls. The aggregate supply curve shifts to the left, from AS to AS₁.

This then gives us our long-run aggregate supply curve, which as the chart shows is vertical. *An increase in aggregate demand as a result of expansionary government policy results in only a temporary increase in output.* Supply-side policies are needed to raise the level of output over the long run – by shifting the long-run AS schedule to the right. Otherwise, expansionary policies result only in higher prices – the final price level is P_3.

Objectives and instruments

Even allowing for this, economic policy does not sound that difficult. Governments just have to make sure that all aspects of policy are geared towards achieving the same **objectives**. These are:

- achievement of the fastest sustainable growth for gross domestic product (GDP)
- the highest possible level of employment

- stable prices (or at least low inflation, for example the current 2.5 per cent target)
- external balance – ensuring the current account of the balance of payments is not in large deficit
- sound public finance – for example the **'golden rule'** of using only public borrowing to finance public investment over the economic cycle.

Governments use **instruments** of policy to achieve these objectives. Macroeconomic policies to boost economic growth include expansionary fiscal policy (reduced taxation and increased government spending) and a relaxation of monetary policy, through lower interest rates and a falling exchange rate. But expanding fiscal policy will mean a bigger budget deficit (or public sector net cash requirement), while lowering both interest rates and the exchange rate would, in normal circumstances, boost inflation.

The government's economic approach

The government's central objective is to achieve high and stable levels of growth and employment, goals which have proved elusive in the past. In meeting this objective, the government wants to encourage a fair society in which everyone can share in higher living standards and greater job opportunities, and to see economic development taking place in a way which respects the environment. Achieving these aims in the new global economy will require a major re-equipping of the British economy.

In working towards its aims, the government is putting in place a comprehensive and consistent set of economic policies designed to:

- *improve the underlying rate of growth and employment* by:
  (a) creating economic stability based on low inflation and low government borrowing
  (b) improving the environment for long-term investment in technology and in education and training
  (c) encouraging a climate of entrepreneurship and competition
- *modernize the welfare state* so that it provides an effective way of supporting people back into work rather than trapping them in poverty
- *ensure high-quality public services* are delivered in the most effective way
- *develop a tax system which is fair* and seen to be fair
- *ensure that economic development takes place* in a way which is consistent with high standards of environmental protection.

Source: Financial Statement and Budget Report, HM Treasury, July 1997

The problem for policymakers is that it is not possible to assign separate policy instruments to the different objectives of policy, and governments typically have more policy objectives than instruments. Jan Tinbergen, a Dutch economist, formulated a 'rule' under which it was necessary to have as many independent policy instruments as objectives. This is why governments have in the past tried to invent new instruments (e.g. prices and incomes policies) which attempt to control inflation directly, in an effort to square the circle.

A bigger problem is that policy instruments operate simultaneously on a number of different targets. A lower exchange rate might be the right policy for achieving balance of payments equilibrium, but it will also (by raising the price of imports) add to inflation.

The modern response to the policy conflict

Modern governments have tried to solve the conflict inherent in objectives and instruments by limiting the scope of macroeconomic policy. The central aim has been to use macroeconomic policy to control inflation, while concentrating the microeconomic policy effort on raising economic growth.

As this approach has been refined, so inflation has come to be the only policy objective which is specifically targeted. Treasury ministers have stressed that the control of inflation has to be the main objective of policy. Without it, growth will inevitably run into the brick wall of an unsustainable balance-of-payments position (British goods become uncompetitive in international markets), and an inevitable tightening of policy to re-establish control over inflation. Low inflation is thus seen as a necessary condition for the achievement of the other objectives. There is no long-run trade-off, in other words, between growth and inflation.

Even with this approach, however, there are compromises. The government does not target zero inflation, but a rate of 2.5 per cent. It also attempts to ensure that the Bank of England does not engage in policy 'overkill'. The Bank is required to explain its actions if inflation falls below 1.5 per cent.

Economic policy, therefore, has to strive to establish a balance between various objectives. Compromises are inevitable, perfection is rarely achieved. If economics is about the allocation of scarce resources, *economic policy is the allocation of scarce policy instruments between competing, and often conflicting, ends.*

KEY WORDS

Gross domestic product
GDP deflator
Retail prices index
RPIX
Unemployment
Balance of payments
Current account
Macroeconomic policy
Fiscal policy
Monetary policy

Microeconomic policy
Supply side
Aggregate demand
Aggregate supply
Keynesian
Neoclassical
Objectives
'Golden rule'
Instruments

Further reading

Bamford, C., and Grant, S., Chapters 1–4 in *The UK Economy in a Global Context,* Heinemann Educational, 2000.

Griffiths, A., and Wall, S., Chapter 17 in *Applied Economics*, 10th edn., Addison Wesley Longman, 2003.

Useful website

HM Treasury: www.hm-treasury.gov.uk/

Essay topics

1. (a) Using a carefully labelled diagram of aggregate demand and aggregate supply, explain what is meant by the equilibrium level of real output. [5 marks]

   (b) Using aggregate demand and supply analysis, outline the effect of each of the following on the equilibrium level of real output:

   (i) A decision by the government to increase substantially its overall expenditure on the National Health Service. [5 marks]

   (ii) The rapid growth of internet technologies providing greater information to firms about the cheapest available supplies of their raw materials. [5 marks]

   (c) Examine the extent to which demand side policies designed to reduce the rate of inflation might cause a rise in the level of unemployment. [15 marks]

   [Edexcel, Q1, Unit 3, Paper 6353, June 2001.]

2. (a) Explain what is meant by a deficit in the current account of the balance of payments. [5 marks]

   (b) Outline the effect of each of the following on economic growth in the United Kingdom:

    (i)   a fall in United Kingdom interest rates [5 marks]
    (ii) a rise in the rate of income tax in the United Kingdom.
                                               [5 marks]
(c) To what extent is it possible for a country to enjoy rapid
economic growth, price stability and an equilibrium on the current
account of its balance of payments? [15 marks]
[Edexcel, Q1, Unit 3, Paper 6353, January 2002

Data response question

Study **Table A** and **Extract A** and then answer **all** parts of the question which follow.

Table A Selected economic indicators

Year	Real consumption expenditure	Rate of interest (%)	Real GDP (£ billion)	Employment (millions)
1989	413	15.2	654	26.2
1990	417	14.0	658	26.4
1991	407	11.0	649	25.9
1992	407	7.3	649	25.3
1993	420	5.3	664	24.9
1994	429	6.6	693	25.1
1995	438	6.5	713	25.4
1996	454	6.4	731	25.6
1997	471	7.6	756	26.1

Source: *The United Kingdom National Accounts and Economic Trends Annual Supplement*, 1998 editions.

Extract A Why is consumer expenditure so important?

Consumption expenditure is the sum of all goods and services produced and sold each year. Consumer expenditure represents around 65% of the Gross Domestic Product (GDP) or the annual output of the economy. It is the largest component of aggregate demand and changes in consumption can have a major impact on output and national income. It follows from this that consumers' decisions can have a significant impact on employment.

Consumer expenditure is strongly influenced by households' disposable income but is also affected by a variety of other factors including consumer confidence, household wealth and taxation. Changes in interest rates introduced by the Monetary Policy Committee of the Bank of England are also likely to have an impact on consumer spending.

Adapted from *Economics Today*, January 1999

(a) Describe the changes in real consumption expenditure which took place between 1989 and 1997 as shown in **Table A**. [5 marks]

(b) Explain how consumer expenditure is likely to be affected by changes in:
  (i) households' disposable income [5 marks]
  (ii) interest rates. [5 marks]

(c) Using the data, discuss the way in which changes in consumer expenditure may have affected output and employment since 1989. [20 marks]

[AQA, Q2 Unit 2, Specimen Paper, 2000]

Chapter Two

Taxation

*'A modern and fair tax system encourages work and saving, keeps
pace with developments in business practice and the global economy
and raises sufficient revenue to fund the government's objective of
establishing world-class public services. To ensure that the burden of
tax does not fall unfairly on compliant taxpayers, loopholes giving
scope for avoidance should be closed. Everyone – individuals and
businesses – should pay their fair share.'*
Pre-Budget Report, HM Treasury, November 2002.

The tax burden

More than 200 years ago, Benjamin Franklin observed that nothing in
this world was more certain 'except death and taxes'. A modern version
of this might be that nothing is more certain than that higher public
spending means, ultimately, higher taxation.

Governments, even those determined to cut public spending and
reduce taxation, have found it difficult to do so. Public spending has
tended to rise as a proportion of GDP, as we shall see in Chapter 3, and
this has meant a rising **tax burden**.

Although opinion polls regularly show that majority public opinion
would accept higher taxation to fund, for example, additional
education and health spending, governments that raise taxes tend to be
unpopular. Starting with Margaret Thatcher's election victory in 1979,
the Conservative party's strongest card was its pledge to reduce
taxation. This continued until the 1992 election when, under John
Major, the party's election manifesto said: 'A lightly taxed economy
generates more economic growth, and more revenue. High taxes kill
the goose that lays the golden eggs.' Unfortunately for the
Conservatives, the next two years saw the biggest tax rises in Britain's
peacetime history, as the government attempted to reduce a budget
deficit swelled by recession – which reduces the growth of tax revenues
– and rapid growth in public spending. The Conservatives lost their
reputation as a low-tax party.

There was still widespread mistrust of the Labour party, however.
One of the reasons for the party's defeat in the 1992 general election
had been its tax plans, in particular an intention to increase income tax
rates for the better off. Although only a minority of people pay the top

rate of income tax, currently 40 per cent, many more people aspire to being well enough off to do so.

Thus, prior to the 1997 general election, Gordon Brown, as shadow chancellor, pledged not to increase either the basic (23 per cent) or top (40 per cent) rate of income tax or to increase value-added tax (17.5 per cent). He also promised that, when circumstances permitted, a Labour government would introduce a reduced rate of income tax of 10 per cent on the first slice of taxable income. This was introduced in 1999 on the first £1500 of taxable income. Under the Conservatives this reduced rate was 20 per cent. In April 2000 the basic rate was reduced to 22 per cent.

The dilemma, however, remains. How is it possible to meet growing demand for higher public expenditure and at the same time reduce, or at least not increase, taxation, in order to reward hard work, responsibility and success through the tax system?

UK could face £11bn budget hole

The UK government may have to raise taxes by up to £11bn a year from 2005 onwards, an independent economic think tank has warned.

Chancellor Gordon Brown can take short-term solace from the fact that the Institute for Fiscal Studies (IFS) believes he will more or less meet his borrowing targets during the next two financial years. But from 2005 onwards the government may have to borrow up to £28bn a year, well above the Chancellor's current forecast of £19bn.

According to the IFS, this will bring the government into conflict with its 'golden' budget rule – which states that it is ok to borrow to invest, but that any additional debt must be repaid over the economic cycle.

If the Chancellor wants to stick to his spending promises on public services like health and education, he will have to increase taxes.

Income tax rise of 4p?

Just to break even he will have to raise his tax take by at least £4bn, and possibly by up to £11bn to have a safety margin, calculate the institute's tax experts.

That is equivalent to a tax rise of between 1p and almost 4p on the basic rate of income tax.

'There is a danger of the Chancellor missing the golden rule as we go forward,' said IFS director Robert Chote when he presented the institute's closely watched Green Budget, which analyses the government's fiscal options.

And if the economy grows slower than currently forecast by the Treasury, the budget shortfall could be even higher.

Source: www.news.bbc.co.uk, 29 January 2003

Direct and indirect taxation

Direct taxation refers to those taxes levied mainly on income. Individuals pay income tax and National Insurance Contributions (NICs) on their earnings. Companies pay corporation tax on profits.

Indirect taxation is levied, not on income, but on spending. Value-added tax (VAT) is one indirect tax, others include the excise duties on petrol, alcohol and tobacco.

Direct taxes are usually **progressive** in that the higher an individual's earnings, or the greater a company's profits, the more tax is paid. Above a certain threshold of income, for example, people pay a higher rate of income tax, currently 40 per cent. Indirect taxation is less progressive, and can be **regressive** – a poor person buying a packet of cigarettes pays the same tax as a rich person. Governments have, however, tried to introduce a progressive element into indirect taxation. Food, children's clothing and other necessities are zero-rated for VAT purposes, while household gas and electricity carries a 5 per cent rate, in comparison with the normal 17.5 per cent rate. These necessities make up a larger proportion of the spending of low-income households.

A perfectly **proportionate** tax system would be one in which people paid the same proportion in taxation, whatever their income level.

Hypothecated taxes are raised for a specific purpose. A tax on road-users used only on building of new roads would be a hypothecated tax.

The principles of taxation

More than 200 years after the publication of *The Wealth of Nations* (1776), Adam Smith's four 'canons' of taxation continue to form the basis of modern tax systems. They are:

- taxes should be based on the ability to pay
- taxes should be easy and cheap to collect
- the method of paying taxes should be convenient for taxpayers
- there should be certainty in the system, with taxpayers knowing how much they need to pay, and when.

Later economists have also stressed the need for taxes to be flexible – capable of being altered to meet new circumstances.

Taxation, incentives and the supply side

Legend has it that the supply-side revolution began in the USA in the 1970s when Professor Arthur Laffer drew his famous **Laffer curve** on a napkin for a journalist from the *Wall Street Journal*. As Figure 4 demonstrates, it showed that, beyond a certain level, higher tax rates

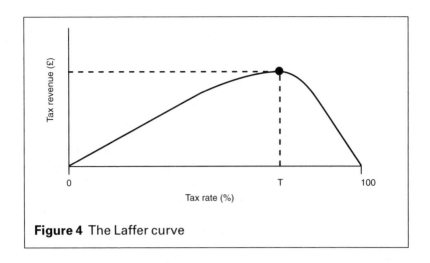

Figure 4 The Laffer curve

will produce a diminishing amount of government revenue, because people have a disincentive to work, and because they, and their accountants, have an incentive to seek out ways of avoiding tax.

In the 1980s in Britain such considerations were a prime factor in reductions in the top marginal rate of income tax from 83 to 40 per cent, and in the basic rate from 33 to 25 (later 22) per cent.

In fact the evidence, both theoretical and empirical, for such incentive effects is thin. It comes down to a basic question: When tax rates fall do people work harder, because they keep a greater share of their income? Or do they work less hard, because by working fewer hours they can keep the same level of after-tax income.

Attempts to study this puzzle empirically have mostly concluded that the majority of people do not have the ability to vary their working hours (or their salary does not vary according to the hours they work). For those who can vary their hours, such as owner-managers, separating lower tax rates from other factors has proved difficult. The theoretical argument is as follows.

Consider Figure 5. 'Indifference curve I' reflects combinations of income and hours of leisure about which the individual is indifferent – he or she cannot choose between them. To accept fewer hours of leisure, the person would require an ever-increasing amount of income to compensate, and vice versa. The individual's chosen combination of work and leisure is reached when indifference curve I just touches the sloping budget line, which joins the Y and L axes. He or she chooses L hours of leisure (the remainder being working time) for an income level Y.

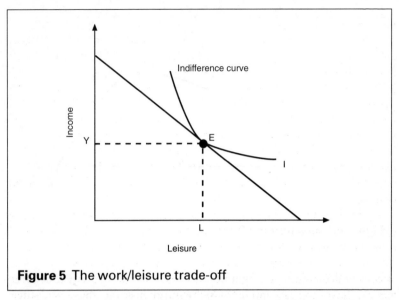

Figure 5 The work/leisure trade-off

One possible effect of reductions in tax rates is shown in Figure 6. Lower tax rates have the effect of steepening the budget line – for every hour worked (and thus for every hour of leisure foregone) the amount of after-tax income is greater than before. In this example, the new

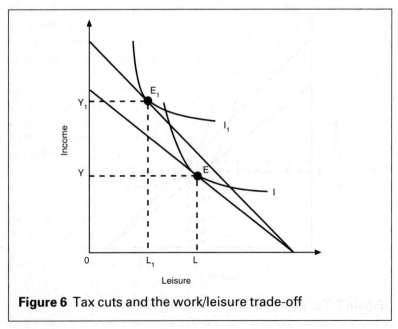

Figure 6 Tax cuts and the work/leisure trade-off

indifference curve which touches the budget line is I_1, and this generates a smaller amount of leisure hours (L_1 instead of L) – and thus a greater amount of hours worked – for a higher income, Y_1 instead of Y. Lower tax rates have thus produced positive incentive effects – longer hours are worked. This is not, however, the only possibility.

Consider now Figure 7, which shows an alternative possibility. If the indifference curve which touches the budget line is I_2, then the effect of a cut in taxes is to produce an increase in the amount of leisure hours from L to L_2, and therefore a reduction in hours worked. In this example, the individual gets the best of both worlds. He or she ends up with a slightly higher income, Y_2, than before but for a smaller number of hours worked.

So which is it more likely to be? There are two distinct effects from a tax cut – the **substitution effect** and the **income effect**. The cut in tax rates has made each hour worked more valuable to the individual, and thus increased the opportunity cost of leisure time. This substitution effect should encourage people to substitute hours of work for hours of leisure, as was the case in Figure 6. Pulling against this, however, is the income effect, in which the individual can work fewer hours for the same, or even for a higher income, than before. Leisure is a 'normal good', demand for which increases as income rises.

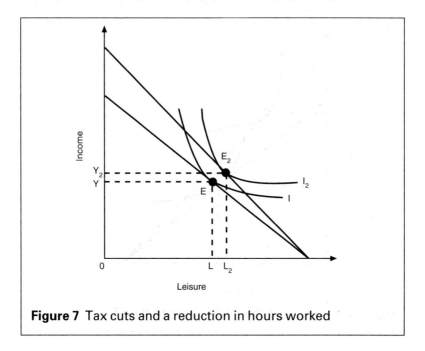

Figure 7 Tax cuts and a reduction in hours worked

Which of these two effects will dominate, and therefore whether or not people will work harder or take it easier, will depend on individual circumstances and preferences.

Taxation and the distribution of income

While the primary purpose of taxation is for governments to raise the

---

Fairness for families

The government is committed to building a fairer and more inclusive society in which everyone can contribute to, and benefit from, rising national prosperity.

The government is reforming the tax and benefit system to tackle child poverty and ensure decent family incomes. The reforms ensure that support is available to all families with children, in recognition of the costs and responsibilities which come with parenthood. Those who need the greatest support, including families on lower incomes, those with children under one, and parents of disabled children, receive the most help.

Since 1997, financial support for families with children has been increased significantly. Reforms so far include:

- record increases in Child Benefit to £15.75 a week for the first child and £10.55 for subsequent children. As announced in Budget 2002, from April 2003, the rates of Child Benefit will rise in line with indexation to £16.05 and £10.75 respectively;
- the introduction of the Children's Tax Credit in April 2001, now worth up to £529 extra a year for around 4.6 million families and, since April 2002, up to £1,049 a year for families in the year of a child's birth;
- the introduction of the Working Families' Tax Credit (WFTC) which benefits over 1.3 million families - around 500,000 more than previously received Family Credit. On average, these families are now receiving over £40 a week more under the WFTC than under Family Credit; and
- increases in the children's allowances in Income Support and other income-related benefits, including a doubling in real terms of the rates for children under 11.

As part of the next steps in tax and benefit reform, Budget 2002 introduced a new system of support to help families, tackle child poverty and make work pay. This includes the introduction, from April 2003, of the new Child Tax Credit from April 2003 to provide a single, seamless system of income-related support for families with children.

As a result of the government's personal tax and benefit reforms since 1997, including the changes to national insurance contributions and the income tax personal allowance announced in Budget 2002, by April 2003:

- families with children will be, on average, £1,200 a year better off, while those in the poorest fifth of the population will be, on average, over £2,400 a year better off in real terms;
- a single-earner family with two young children on half average earnings of £14,100 will be £3,490 a year better off in real terms; and
- a single-earner family on average earnings of £28,200 and with two children will be £310 a year better off in real terms.

Source: www.hm-treasury.gov.uk, March 2003

revenues needed to finance public spending, an important secondary objective, in modern times, has been the *redistribution of income.*

In the 1970s, when Labour was previously in power, not only was the overall tax burden higher as a percentage of GDP, but the tax system was heavily progressive. The basic rate of income tax was 33 per cent but the highest marginal rate was 83 per cent. Above a certain level of income, in other words, people would keep only 17 pence from every extra pound they earned.

This changed significantly under the Conservative government elected in 1979. The basic rate of income tax was cut to 30 per cent, and the top rate to 60 per cent, financed by an increase in VAT from 8 per cent and 12.5 per cent to a uniform rate of 15 per cent. The tax system was thus made more regressive at a stroke. The Conservatives persisted with this strategy, eventually reducing the top rate of income tax to 40 per cent and the basic rate to 23 per cent, while raising VAT further, to 17.5 per cent. The period of Conservative rule, and particularly the 1980s, saw a sharp rise in income inequality in Britain.

The dilemma for the Labour party in the run-up to the May 1997 general election was that, while many of its supporters favoured using the tax system to take money away from 'fat cats' and redistribute it to people on low incomes, the party leadership feared an adverse response from voters towards any plan for raising income tax rates. Thus, Labour went into the election pledging not to increase income tax rates or VAT.

In practice the Blair government has tried to redistribute income in other ways, by taxing share dividends more heavily, and by introducing a new tax 'credit' – the working families' tax credit (to be renamed the working tax credit)– designed to help people on lower incomes. Later it introduced a new child tax credit. It has also concentrated its tax-cutting agenda on a new lower starting rate of income tax, of 10 per cent.

Other tax changes have, however, been unfavourable to those on low incomes – for example the decision to raise the excise duties on petrol by 6 per cent a year in real terms, with a similar increase for cigarette duties. Both impact disproportionately on lower-income households.

In April 2002, Labour announced significant increases in overall taxation, to take effect in 2003. The centrepiece of these tax increases was a 1 per cent increase in both employer and employee National Insurance contributions. This measure alone raised £8 billion a year, to pay for improvements in public services.

Tax policy in practice: the budget

The budget, which is presented in March, sets out the government's tax

Table 2 Government receipts in 2002–03 (£ billion)

Inland Revenue	
Income tax	114.1
Corporation tax	29.3
Tax credits	–3.5
Petroleum revenue tax	1.1
Capital gains tax	2.0
Inheritance tax	2.4
Stamp duties	8.2
Customs & Excise	
Value-added tax	64.5
Fuel duties	22.4
Tobacco duties	8.2
Alcohol duties	7.2
Others	7.8
Social security contributions and others	
Social security contributions	65.5
Business rates	18.0
Council tax	16.6
Vehicle excise duties	4.4
Others	11.4
Total (tax and social security)	379.6

Source: Pre-Budget Report, HM Treasury, November 2002

plans for the coming fiscal year beginning in April. Prior to that, each November, the chancellor publishes a pre-budget report, or 'green' budget (as in Green Paper) which sets out tax options for the following spring.

Under the Conservatives from 1993 to 1997, there was a 'unified' November budget, setting out both tax and public expenditure plans. The Labour government decided, however, to set three-year spending plans for government departments, so the annual budget is now concerned with taxation.

Some changes occur automatically at budget time. Examples are the '**indexation**' (increasing in line with inflation) of most tax allowances and some excise duties, such as on alcohol. Other decisions are known as **discretionary tax changes**, when the Chancellor raises or lowers taxes to meet the government's objectives. Table 2 shows the main sources of government tax revenues.

Tax harmonization in Europe

An important issue both now and in the future is the **harmonization** of taxes within Europe.

When the Labour government took power in May 1997 it pledged to remove value-added tax on domestic fuel and power (gas and electricity bills), introduced by the previous Conservative government. However, it was soon discovered that, under EU rules, VAT on fuel could not be removed entirely but only reduced, to 5 per cent. This is because VAT rates have been harmonized in Europe. Why is this?

Imagine two neighbouring countries, with no trade barriers or restrictions on the movement of people between them. One has a VAT rate of 5 per cent on goods, the other sets a rate of 20 per cent. People from the high-VAT country would cross the border to buy all their goods in the low-VAT country. The former would lose tax revenue and its economy would suffer. The latter would gain on both counts.

Thus in 1992, ahead of the start of the European 'single market' at the end of that year, finance ministers in Europe agreed on a minimum standard rate of VAT of 15 per cent (fuel, food and other essentials can be taxed at a lower rate but again within preset limits). The new minimum rate of VAT did not eliminate all variations – VAT rates currently range from 15 per cent in Luxembourg to 25 per cent in Sweden and Denmark – but it reduced them. The experience of the USA, where individual states operate different rates of sales tax, suggests that a single market does not require complete harmonization of taxes.

Pressure for greater harmonization of other taxes – on investment, on companies, and even on income – has been quite strong within Europe. It is argued, for example, that countries offering lower rates of corporation tax are providing an unfair incentive for companies to locate there. Similarly, countries offering lower income tax rates, particularly for higher earners, can be said to be offering a powerful incentive to managers to locate their businesses there.

Harmonization of taxes can be expected to increase in Europe. The Chancellor has faced pressure from the tobacco and drinks industries to reduce the excise duties on cigarettes and alcohol, because of the loss of business to the so-called 'Calais run', where people can buy cheaper in northern France, where duty levels are far lower.

Perfect harmonization of taxes is, however, unlikely. Some countries in Europe raise much more tax as a percentage of GDP than do others. Portugal, for example, raises only 34.5 per cent of its GDP in tax, compared with 53.2 per cent in Sweden.

> ## KEY WORDS
>
> | | |
> |---|---|
> | Tax burden | Laffer curve |
> | Direct taxation | Substitution effect |
> | Indirect taxation | Income effect |
> | Progressive | Indexation |
> | Regressive | Discretionary tax changes |
> | Proportionate | Harmonization |
> | Hypothecated taxes | |

Further reading

Bamford, C., and Grant, S., Chapter 3 in *The UK Economy in a Global Context*, Heinemann Educational, 2000.

Cook, M., and Healey, N., Chapter 5 in *Supply Side Policies*, 4th edn., Heinemann Educational, 2001.

Grant, S., and Vidler, C., AS Section 4 Unit 27 and A2 Section 4 Unit 19 in *Economics in Context*, Heinemann, 2000.

Smith, D., Chapter 13 in *Free Lunch*, Profile Books, 2003.

Useful website

Institute for Fiscal Studies: www.ifs.org.uk/

Essay topics

1. (a) Explain how a decrease in income tax rates can lead to a multiple increase in national income. [10 marks]

   (b) Discuss whether a decrease in income tax rates or an increase in government expenditure would be more effective in reducing unemployment. [15 marks]

2. Assess the arguments for and against shifting the burden of taxation from direct to indirect taxes. [25 marks]

Data response question

In his April 2003 budget, Gordon Brown, the Chancellor of the Exchequer, increased excise duty on cigarettes by 8p a packet, on beer by 1p a pint, and on wine by 4p a bottle but froze the tax on spirits and sparkling wine. The UK drinks and tobacco industry predicted that these changes would lead to increased demand for 'booze cruises' to France and Belgium and an increase in sales by smugglers.

The Chancellor did not raise income tax rates but he did freeze the personal tax allowance. He also announced he would only impose a 1.28p per litre increase on petrol if the oil price stabilized. He increased vehicle excise duty for cars by £5 from May 1 but froze the rate for lorries and motorcycles. The tax disc for cars with the lowest fuel consumption was cut to £55. Over the period 2001 to 2003 fuel duty actually fell in real terms.

Since he became Chancellor in May 1997, Gordon Brown has made a number of tax changes designed to improve the supply-side of the economy. These have included corporation tax cuts, lower capital gains tax on business assets, a simplified VAT system for small firms and cuts in income tax.

The Chancellor's tax and benefit changes have made income more evenly distributed. The poorest ten per cent of people have seen their incomes rise by 15 per cent whilst the richest are worse off by three per cent.

(a) Identify a direct tax and an indirect tax mentioned in the passage. [2 marks]
(b) Explain two arguments for increasing excise duty on cigarettes. [6 marks]
(c) What information is there in the passage which could be used in support of tax harmonization within the EU? [4 marks]
(d) Analyse one argument against reducing fuel duty in real terms. [3 marks]
(e) Explain two fiscal policy measures a government could use to reduce income inequality. [6 marks]
(f) Discuss how one of the tax changes mentioned in the passage could improve the supply-side of the economy. [4 marks]

Chapter Three

Public expenditure and the changing role of fiscal policy

'Sound finance may be right psychologically, but economically it is a depressing influence.' John Maynard Keynes

'The government's fiscal policy objectives are:
- *over the medium-term, to ensure sound public finances and that spending and taxation impact fairly within and between generations; and*
- *over the short term, to support monetary policy and, in particular, to allow the automatic stabilizers to help smooth the path of the economy.*

These objectives are implemented through two fiscal rules:
- *the golden rule: over the economic cycle, the government will borrow only to invest and not to fund current spending; and*
- *the sustainable investment rule: public sector net debt as a proportion of GDP will be held over the economic cycle at a stable and prudent level. Other things being equal, net debt will be maintained below 40 per cent of GDP over the economic cycle.'*

Pre-Budget Report, HM Treasury, November 2002

Fiscal policy and the growth of public spending

Fiscal means 'pertaining to public revenue' – in other words taxation. **Fiscal policy,** however, refers to both sides of government accounts, revenue and expenditure. The growth of public expenditure throughout much of the twentieth century ensured an enhanced role for fiscal policy. This growth has occurred in stages.

● Victorian values

In the early years of the century, taxation and public spending were equivalent to roughly 10 per cent of gross domestic product (GDP) and governments typically ran a **budget surplus** because tax revenues exceeded public spending. Throughout the Victorian and early Edwardian era, governments aimed to repay some of the **national debt.**

● Keynes and the Great Depression

The First World War (1914–18) increased the national debt and was followed by substantially higher public expenditure. This was due not only to the early stages of the modern **welfare state**, but also to the influence of John Maynard Keynes, who argued for higher government spending as a solution to the Great Depression. Public spending was typically 20 per cent of GDP or more in the inter-war years.

● The modern welfare state

During the Second World War (1939–45) the government had taken a much bigger role in the economy. This was continued by the 1945–51 Labour administration led by Attlee. The modern welfare state, based on the **Beveridge Report** of 1942, came into being. The National Health Service (NHS) was created in 1948. More than 20 per cent of industry was taken into public ownership, including coal, rail, road freight, civil aviation, gas, electricity, iron and steel. The government accepted the prescriptions of Keynes, committing itself to full employment, and state intervention to achieve that end.

The direct influence of government increased. From 30–40 per cent of GDP in the 1950s and 60s, government spending rose to the equivalent of 40–50 per cent of GDP in the period from the 1970s to the 90s, even under Margaret Thatcher's Conservative government, which was committed to 'rolling back the frontiers of the state'.

ıring the 1990s, however, public spending was brought back under :rol. Some economists predict that increasing demand for public ices and the pressures of an ageing population will lead to an inevitable rise in spending as a proportion of GDP. After taking office in 1997, the Labour government initially kept very tight control on public expenditure, and its share of GDP fell further. But in January 2000 the Prime Minister pledged to increase National Health Service

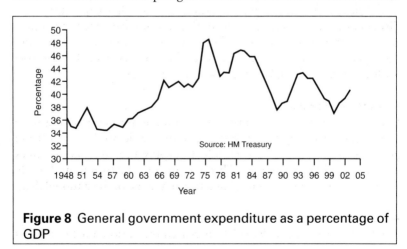

Figure 8 General government expenditure as a percentage of GDP

spending to the EU average. This was followed in 2002 with further big increases in NHS spending – an annual rise in real spending of 7.4 per cent a year for five years – as well as spending on other programmes such as education, and a promised rise in spending on the transport infrastructure. The result was a planned rise in the public spending share of GDP from 37.4 per cent in 1999–2000 to 41.9 per cent in 2005–06. Figure 8 shows the post-war record.

Spending and transfers

In considering the level of public expenditure, it is necessary to distinguish between direct spending by government, for example on the police, the armed forces, or road-building, and **transfers**.

Transfers, such as pensions, the jobseekers' allowance and other social security benefits, do not represent direct spending by

Brown's tax and spend 'gamble' under attack

By BENEDICT BROGAN, Political Correspondent

Tony Blair has 'gambled' on an economy based on tax and spend that has sent the national tax bill soaring but has failed to deliver improvements in public services, Iain Duncan Smith said last night.

In a speech to company executives in the City, the Conservative leader called on the public to use the next election to throw out Labour before Gordon Brown 'steers the country on to the rocks'.

Mr Duncan Smith said the amount taken in tax would have risen from £270 billion when Labour came to power in 1997 to £405 billion by next year. 'The price per household for government services has gone up from £11,000 to £16,500 a year. Does it feel like a 50 per cent improvement?'

The Tories seized on the disclosure that the Budget had been pushed back to the first week in April. They accused Mr Brown of using the cover of loom-

ing war in Iraq to hide possible tax rises.

Mr Duncan Smith called on the Chancellor to reconsider his decision to increase National Insurance by a penny in the pound next month.

'The government has gambled its entire economic strategy on an assumption that it can continue to take more and more tax – currently £109 billion more – and that businesses and people can continue to afford it.

'Labour should pay the price at the next election by being thrown out.'

The International Monetary Fund said yesterday that Mr Brown must put up taxes and slow his spending increases to avoid deepening the hole in Treasury finances.

The IMF's annual report on the UK economy said Mr Brown's assumptions for economic growth 'appear optimistic' as tax revenues, especially from the City, were falling.

The Daily Telegraph, 4 March 2003

government. Instead, they represent a transfer from one set of people – taxpayers – to another set, claimants.

Many taxpayers, indeed, also receive benefits. Pensioners with a private pension as well as the basic state pension are taxpayers. So too are taxpaying households who receive, say, child benefit.

Economists distinguish between direct government spending and transfers. The former is a direct claim by government on the nation's resources and is about 20 per cent of the UK's GDP. The latter is a form of redistribution but, once the transfer has been made, the government has no control over the way the money is spent.

In practical terms the level of transfers is important because it affects the level of taxation. The rising share of taxation as a proportion of GDP in modern times has largely been due to rising social security payments. Governments wishing to hold down taxation therefore need to control social security payments. To the extent that such payments rise, for example, when unemployment goes up, this is difficult. There is, however, certain action the government can take. Soon after being elected in 1979, the Thatcher government linked the annual uprating of state pensions and other social security benefits to prices (the retail prices index) rather than to earnings, which tend to rise faster. By the 1990s, this measure was saving several billion pounds a year.

In March 1999, the Chancellor announced that a minimum income guarantee for pensioners would rise in line with earnings rather than prices.

Debts and deficits

The *national debt* is the amount of borrowing that the government has accumulated over time. There are two ways of measuring this debt.

- Net public sector debt stood at £332 billion, or 31 per cent of GDP in 2002/03.
- General government gross debt, which is used for the purposes of the Maastricht conditions for European economic and monetary union, was £396 billion, or 37.9 per cent of GDP. Under the Maastricht treaty it was required to be 60 per cent of GDP or below.

The difference between these two figures for debt is that the former is reduced by the amount of the government's short-term financial assets, such as bank deposits and foreign currency reserves.

The *budget deficit* (or surplus) is the difference between government spending and tax receipts in any one year. There are several ways of measuring the budget deficit or surplus.

For many years the **public sector borrowing requirement** (PSBR) was the most commonly used measure. More recently, this has been renamed the **public sector net cash requirement** (PSNCR). The government currently stresses other measures, notably **net borrowing** and the **current budget surplus/deficit**. It is not necessary to concern ourselves with the precise detail of these definitions.

When governments run a budget deficit, or borrow, fiscal policy is expansionary; and vice versa when governments run a surplus, or repay debt. There is, however, one important proviso. This is that budget deficits are a normal consequence of economic downturns – tax revenues decline and public spending on unemployment benefits increases – while the budget will tend towards a surplus when economic growth is strong. Economists sometimes call these effects the **automatic stabilizers**. It is important in judging whether economic policy is expansionary or contractionary to assess the position of the economy in the economic cycle.

Deficits and 'crowding out'

Why do governments need to control budget deficits? One reason, which the government cited during the 1980s when monetarism was in vogue, was that government borrowing added to the growth of the money supply and was therefore considered to be inflationary. A more traditional reason is that borrowing by governments now means that future generations will be left with the burden of repaying that debt – there is an **inter-generational transfer** of the tax burden. Future generations will have to pay higher taxes to fund public spending now.

A third reason is called **financial crowding out**. The more that the government borrows by issuing UK government bonds (called 'gilts' because the certificates used to have a gilt-edged border), the more – given a limited supply of funds – interest rates will be forced higher, discouraging private sector firms from borrowing to invest. The public sector is thus crowding out the private sector. In 2001 and 2002, thanks to low levels of government borrowing, low inflation and weak stock markets, long-term interest rates on UK gilts fell to their lowest level for more than 30 years. Thus, the public sector was leaving room for the private sector to borrow and invest.

Keynesians, it should be said, dispute this. They argue that 'crowding in' is a more powerful effect. When the government invests, they argue, this gives the business world the confidence to do so as well.

The composition of public spending

The composition of public spending has changed significantly in the post-war period. In 1950, in the wake of the Second World War, the

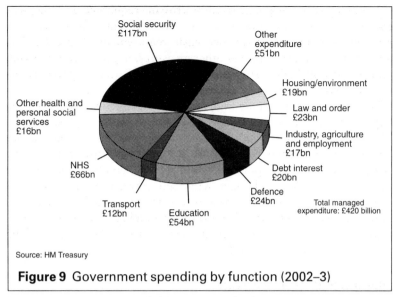

Source: HM Treasury

Figure 9 Government spending by function (2002–3)

biggest programme was defence (with a budget equivalent to 6.6 per cent of GDP), followed by social security (5.1 per cent), health (3.6 per cent), education (3.4 per cent) and housing (2.6 per cent).

Fifty years on, the four biggest programmes remain the same, although their order has changed significantly, with social security easily having the biggest budget in 2002–03 (11.2 per cent of GDP), followed by health and personal social services (7.9 per cent), education (5.2 per cent) and defence (2.3 per cent).

Government spending on housing has declined sharply, because of the rise in owner-occupation and the sale of a large part of the council housing stock to the public under the right-to-buy legislation. Figure 9 summarizes the recent position.

The comprehensive spending review

One significant change introduced by the Labour government elected in 1997 was to conduct a **comprehensive spending review**. This was to ensure that spending was being directed to the areas the government considered were its main priorities.

Also, and significantly, spending limits were to be agreed for all government departments for a three-year period, both to provide individual departments with greater certainty for planning purposes, and to prevent the normal sharp pre-election rise in government outlays. Economists have long observed that public spending tends to rise, and tax rates fall, in the run-up to general elections.

The main outcomes of the third review, announced in July 2002, were:

- current spending will rise in total by 3.3 per cent a year in real terms in 2004–05 and 2005–06
- public sector net investment is projected to rise from its 1.8 per cent of GDP target in 2003–04, to 2 per cent of GDP by 2005–06 and to 2.25 per cent by 2007–08
- UK spending on the NHS will increase by an average of 7.4 per cent a year in real terms over the five years to 2007–08
- Over 75 per cent of the additional spending will be allocated to the key priorities of health, education, personal social services, transport, housing and criminal justice.

A new political consensus on public spending?

Before the 1997 general election, many Conservative politicians favoured reducing public spending as a share of GDP.

It was argued that in very prosperous economies in the world, such as the USA, public spending was only around 30 per cent of GDP compared with 40 per cent in the UK and 50 per cent in many other European countries. The argument was that lower levels of public spending permit lower taxation, and that this provides individuals and businesses with greater 'supply-side' incentives, as discussed in the previous chapter.

Many Conservatives also argued that, such were the likely future pressures on the NHS and social security spending as a result of an ageing population – older people require more healthcare spending and the amount that would have to be paid out in state pensions would increase – it would be necessary to find private-sector ways of funding long-term care for the elderly, and of encouraging a higher proportion of people to take out private pensions. The Conservatives were also keen to encourage private education.

This party policy changed in 1999 when Peter Lilley, in a speech as deputy leader of the Conservative party, said there was only a limited role for the private sector in providing for these various aspects of the welfare state (health, education and social security) and that a future Conservative government would recognize this. Francis Maude, the shadow chancellor, also pledged that a Conservative government would match the spending increases on health and education by the Labour government.

Although this appeared to signal a truce in the debate over the size of the state, there was another shift after the 2001 election. When Labour announced significant increases in government spending, to more than

40 per cent of GDP, the Conservatives under Iain Duncan Smith claimed that they could achieve improvements in public services without spending so much and also that the party remained wedded to tax cuts.

Privatization

If you asked an international audience what was the most notable economic policy to have come out of Britain in the past 20 years or so, they would probably say **privatization**. Privatization, nowadays less frequently known as denationalization or **asset sales,** means in its most straightforward form precisely that – the sale of state assets to the private sector.

Between 1979 and 1997, Conservative governments sold 46 previously state-owned companies to the private sector (accounting for 900 000 jobs), including British Telecom, British Gas, the water, electricity and railway industries, British Airways, BAA (formerly the British Airports Authority), British Steel and Girobank.

It is difficult to overstate the scale of this change. It reflects a shift in philosophy from a belief that utilities providing the basics of life – water, electricity, gas, public transport – should be monopoly state suppliers, to a belief that these things are better run by the private sector. It was also lucrative for the government – asset sales raised nearly £70 billion between 1979 and 1997, although subsequently the government was accused of selling them off too cheaply. An unusual privatization occurred in 2000, when the government sold the so-called radio spectrum for third generation (3G) mobile phones, raising £22.5 billion.

Privatization can also, however, be widened to include other policy actions which allow the private sector into areas that were previously the exclusive domain of the state.

● Deregulation

Deregulation is the removal of legal and other barriers to entry into industries previously dominated by public provision. Bus deregulation allowed private operators into a market in which state or council-run services had dominated.

● Franchising

Franchising is the opening up of services previously provided 'in-house' by the public sector, through **compulsory competitive tendering**. Councils were required to allow private companies to tender for services they previously operated themselves, such as refuse collection.

● The private finance initiative

The **private finance initiative** (PFI), or public/private partnerships, arise when the public sector purchases services from a private sector partner. The private partner has generally undertaken the capital investment, for example the building of a new hospital or road, and the public sector pays for the use of that facility.

The value of the PFI for the government is that investment occurs which would previously have been constrained by the state of the public finances – tax or borrowing would have had to rise to fund the investment. The government set a target of more than £12 billion for PFI contracts over the three-year period from 2002–03. Private sector investment through such contracts is equivalent to about 10 per cent of annual investment each year.

The case for and against privatization

In examining the case for privatization, it is worth recalling first why some activities were thought to be best performed by the state, or by state-owned corporations.

Arguments in favour of state control

The arguments in favour of state control were as follows:

● There are **natural monopolies** such as gas, electricity, water and the railways, where unit costs decline with increased output, and where competition would mean wasteful duplication of services. Allowing a private firm to run such natural monopolies would mean they benefited from excess monopoly profits.

● Where firms are state-owned, it is easier to deal directly with **externalities**, such as pollution from power stations.

● Certain large **high-risk projects**, which are indivisible (they cannot be broken up into smaller amounts of investment) would be difficult to finance privately. If you want to create a national electricity grid, for example, it is easier to spread the cost across all taxpayers.

● Nationalized industries, it was thought, would have better **industrial relations**, because workers would be less willing to take industrial action against organizations that they, as taxpayers, ultimately owned. For similar reasons it was thought that **productivity** (output per worker) would be higher in state-owned industries.

● State-owned industries could be used in support of government macroeconomic policy, by maintaining or increasing employment during times of recession.

● Nationalized industries could pursue investment and other strategies in the long-term interests of the country, whereas private firms were subject to pressures for short-term profit maximization – and could be punished by going out of business if they failed to provide what customers wanted.

Many of these arguments proved to be mistaken in practice. The industrial relations climate in nationalized industries was worse than in the private sector, because workers believed that such was the strategic importance of their industries and so large the public purse, strike action would normally bring rewards. Productivity was lower in the public sector, partly because of poor management. Investment, far from being easier to undertake, was subject to political constraints. The current private finance initiative is a recognition of the fact that, contrary to the theory, it is often easier for the private sector to finance large-scale 'public' investments.

Arguments in favour of privatization
There are several separate arguments in favour of privatization:

- *Incentives*. Private sector managers and directors have the carrot of being directly rewarded when profits improve.
- *Punishment*. Dismissal is the private sector penalty when things go badly. It is less likely to be the case within nationalized industries.
- *Political interference*. Decisions can be forced on nationalized industries by ministers for short-term political gain. The private sector has a freer hand.
- *Access to capital*. Private firms can raise funds for expansion from shareholders, whereas nationalized industries often come up against unrealistic Treasury targets for the rate of return on capital projects, or are constrained by public borrowing considerations from raising finance.

Privatization and regulation
One persistent criticism of privatization, as carried out by Conservative governments, is that it transferred monopolies from the public sector to the private sector, allowing excess profits to be made. The response to this has been **regulation**, requiring the privatized utilities to maintain a specified level of service (including uneconomic aspects of the business) and controlling their prices. Within this the privatized utilities would then be free to achieve maximum profits.

Typically, under a formula devised by Professor Stephen Littlechild – who subsequently became the regulator for the electricity industry – privatized firms were required to set annual price rises on the basis of an '**RPI minus** x' formula. This meant that they could raise prices by no more than a specified amount (x) below the inflation rate (measured by the RPI, or retail prices index).

Thus, if inflation was 4.5 per cent, and x was 2 per cent, the maximum the industry would be able to raise prices was 2.5 per cent.

This formula was used by Oftel, the telecommunications regulator, set up on the privatization of BT in 1984, and by Ofgas, as gas regulator, and Offer, the electricity regulator. Ofwat, set up to regulate the privatized water industry, was the exception, setting an 'RPI *plus k*' formula. Water companies were allowed to raise their prices by *more* than inflation, by the maximum amount k per cent, on the understanding that the additional amount must be used to finance environmental improvements.

On taking office in 1997, the Labour government announced that it was reviewing the regulatory regime, with a view to consolidating the different regulatory bodies into a single large regulator.

The new Labour government also made clear its dissatisfaction with the way the regulatory process had been allowed to operate in the early years after privatization, allowing excess profits to be made. In the July 1997 budget it announced a £5 billion one-off **windfall tax** on the gas, electricity, water and telecommunications industries, to finance the New Deal for the long-term unemployed.

The approach to privatization can be seen to have changed as the policy matured. Initially, companies were sold as monopolies to the private sector, for example in the case of BT, and competition introduced only later. Later privatizations either reduced the period in which the privatized company was allowed to make monopoly profits or achieved the sale in a different way. Rail privatization, for example, did not sell British Rail in its entirety to a single private sector company, but split the sale into the track company, Railtrack, as well as rolling stock companies and a series of train operating companies, running different parts of the network. This did not prevent the charge of, in some cases, excess profit or, in many cases, of poor service. In October 2001, Railtrack was put into administration by the government and replaced by Network Rail, not quite a nationalized firm but a company limited by guarantee and non-profit making.

The National Asset Register

Traditionally Labour governments were in favour of nationalization and Conservative governments went for denationalization, although it was not until after 1979 that privatization occurred on any scale.

By the time the Conservatives had privatized most of the big state-owned corporations, the Labour party's position was that it would not seek to renationalize them, because it would be too expensive to do so and there were other priorities for government spending. In practice, the Labour administration which took office in May 1997 has continued with sales of state assets, partly for the reason that this frees resources to be spent on other government provision.

After the general election the Treasury instructed all government departments to draw up a list of the assets they owned so that surplus assets such as buildings and land could be sold off. Thus was born the **National Asset Register**.

KEY WORDS

Fiscal policy	Privatization
Budget surplus	Asset sales
National debt	Deregulation
Welfare state	Franchising
Beveridge Report	Compulsory competitive
Transfers	tendering
Public sector borrowing	Private finance initiative
requirement	Natural monopolies
Public sector net cash	Externalities
requirement	High-risk projects
Net borrowing	Industrial relations
Current budget surplus	Productivity
Automatic stabilizers	Regulation
Inter-generational transfer	RPI minus x
Financial crowding-out	Windfall tax
Comprehensive spending	National Asset Register
review	

Further reading

Bamford, C., Chapter 5 in *Transport Economics*, 3rd edn., Heinemann Educational, 2001.

Bamford, C., and Grant, S., Chapter 3 in *The UK Economy in a Global Context*, Heinemann Educational, 2000.

Grant, S., and Vidler, C., A2 Section 4 Unit 19 in *Economics in Context*, Heinemann, 2000.

Smith, D., Chapter 9 in *Free Lunch*, Profile Books, 2003.

Useful website

HM Treasury: www.hm-treasury.gov.uk/

Essay topics

1. Changes in UK fiscal policy instruments could have an impact on

income distribution, the size of the government's borrowing requirement and the performance of the economy as a whole.

(a)   Explain the factors that might affect the size of the UK's budget deficit or surplus. [10 marks]

(b)   Discuss the impact of changes in UK fiscal policy on income distribution and on the performance of the economy as a whole. [15 marks]

[OCR, Q4, Paper 2887, June 2003]

2. (a) Explain what is meant by a fall in the rate of inflation and a reduction in the government's budget deficit. [5 marks]

(b) Identify the likely economic costs of:

(i)   a rise in the rate of inflation [5 marks]

(ii) a large budget deficit. [5 marks]

(c) Examine the effectiveness of fiscal policy for a country faced with both high levels of inflation and a large budget deficit. [15 marks]

[Edexcel, Q1, Unit 3, Paper 6353, June 2002]

Data response question

Budget boost for the economy

In the March 2000 Budget, the Chancellor of the Exchequer, Gordon Brown, announced a range of tax changes and increased government spending on education and the National Health Service.

Unexpectedly large tax revenues gave the Chancellor the opportunity of increasing government spending or cutting tax rates or a combination of both. He decided to make only small tax cuts but relatively large increases in government spending.

(5)

Some economists claimed that the boost to aggregate demand caused by Gordon Brown's fiscal policy decisions would force the Bank of England to raise interest rates to slow the economy. They expressed concern that recent interest rate rises had already pushed the value of the pound to a fourteen year high against major European currencies. Any further tightening of monetary policy, they argued, would hit exporters.

(10)

Table A Budget information and forecasts

	1999 (actual)	2001 (forecast)
Economic growth (% per annum)	2	2.25–2.75
Inflation (% per annum)	2.25	2.5
Increase in consumer spending (% per annum)	4	2–2.5
Increase in government spending (% per annum)	3.5	2.75
Increase in investment (% per annum)	5.25	3.75–4.25
Balance of payments: current account (£bn)	–12.25	–21

Source: *The Independent*, 22 March 2000.

(a) (i) Distinguish between fiscal policy and monetary policy. [4 marks]

(ii) Explain one reason why tax revenue may increase when incomes rise. [3 marks]

(b) (i) Describe how economic growth is measured. [4 marks]

(ii) Explain one possible cost of economic growth. [4 marks]

(c) (i) State the components of aggregate demand. [2 marks]

(ii) Explain the effect that an increase in interest rates is likely to have on two of the components of aggregate demand. [6 marks]

(d) The passage mentions a change in government spending (line 2). Using an aggregate demand and supply diagram, analyse the effects of an increase in government spending on output and the price level. [7 marks]

(e) Selecting information from Table A, discuss whether the performance of the UK economy was expected to improve between 1999 and 2001. [10 marks]

[OCR, Paper 2883, January 2001]

Chapter Four

The Bank of England and monetary policy

'The monetary policy framework is delivering low and stable inflation, while allowing the Bank of England's Monetary Policy Committee (MPC) to respond to risks to the symmetrical inflation target. Since its introduction in 1997, the monetary policy framework has consistently delivered inflation close to the government's target. The MPC has responded to developments in the world economy, limiting the impact of global instability on the UK economy.'
Pre Budget Report, HM Treasury, November 2002

What is monetary policy?

Monetary policy and fiscal policy represent the two most important levers for controlling the economy. As we have seen, fiscal policy refers to taxation and public spending. Monetary policy is concerned with setting **monetary conditions** in the economy.

This includes a range of connected factors, most importantly the level of **interest rates,** but also the **exchange rate,** and rates of growth of **money and credit.** In general, a policy of raising interest rates and, in a floating exchange rate regime, allowing the currency value to rise – a **monetary tightening** – would be expected to slow the rate of growth of money and credit, and thus slow the economy. Reducing interest rates would represent a **monetary loosening.**

Monetary policy, like fiscal policy, has changed significantly in emphasis and scope in the post-war period.

- During the 1950s and 60s it was seen as an adjunct to fiscal policy in the task of **demand management.**
- In the 1970s and 80s it became the dominant instrument of *macroeconomic policy,* aimed at the goal of achieving and maintaining low inflation.
- In the 1990s this remained the role of economic policy, with the exception of the period from October 1990 to September 1992, when sterling was in the European **exchange rate mechanism** (ERM) and the pound's level drove monetary policy.

The operation of monetary policy changed significantly in May 1997 when, soon after the Labour party's election victory, the Chancellor of the Exchequer announced **operational independence** for the Bank of England. The government would set an official **inflation target**, currently 2.5 per cent, for the **underlying inflation** rate (measured by the retail prices index excluding mortgage interest payments), but decisions on the level of interest rates to achieve it would be taken independently by the Bank's **monetary policy committee**.

The decision to give the Bank operational independence, discussed in more detail below, was the culmination of a process in which *monetary policy has become the main weapon of short-term economic management, while fiscal policy concentrates on medium- and long-term issues.* Thus, while the level of interest rates can be changed from month to month, tax and public spending changes are much less frequent. The government now sets its public spending plans for three years ahead and tax changes are seen to be most important in the way they influence incentives and the supply side, as well as the distribution of income. Thus, when action has to be taken to boost or slow the economy, the onus is on monetary policy.

How does monetary policy work?

The easiest way of thinking of monetary policy is to remember that the interest rate represents the *price* of money, and that the higher the price the lower the demand. Raising interest rates reduces the **demand for money**, lowering them increases it. The demand for money, or **liquidity preference schedule** in Figure 10, demonstrates this effect. When interest rates are reduced from r_1 to r_2, the demand for money increases and the money supply increases from M_1 to M_2.

How does this work in practice? After all, in an economy there are both borrowers and savers. A fall in interest rates reduces, for example, the monthly mortgage payments of borrowers but it also reduces the income of savers. Why should not these two effects simply cancel one another out?

The reason why lower interest rates boost the economy is that borrowers have a higher **marginal propensity to consume** than savers. A young family with a mortgage is more likely to spend the proceeds of an interest rate reduction than an older person with savings is to increase spending in response to an interest rate rise. Lower interest rates also stimulate investment by companies. For an investment project to be worthwhile, companies have to be sure they can more than cover the cost of their borrowing. The lower the interest rate cost of borrowing, the greater the number of investment projects that will become viable.

In an open economy such as Britain, which trades a high proportion – just over 30 per cent – of GDP, the exchange rate is also an important

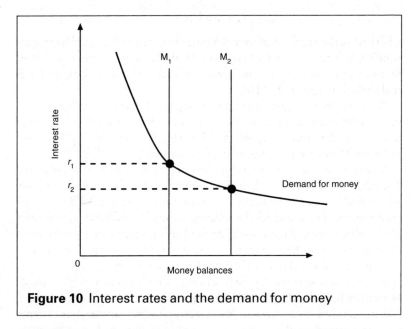

Figure 10 Interest rates and the demand for money

transmission mechanism for monetary policy. A reduction in interest rates will tend to reduce the level of the pound, because it becomes less rewarding for international investors to keep their money in UK assets. A fall in the value of the pound can stimulate economic growth by making it easier for exporters to sell in overseas markets, and for British companies to compete against imports at home.

Monetarism and the role of the money supply

Monetarists believe the money supply is the key variable in the economy. The faster the growth in the money supply, the faster the growth of GDP in money terms. But, since the economy can grow only so far in real terms because of supply-side constraints, eventually too rapid a rate of growth in the money supply will lead to higher inflation.

Milton Friedman, perhaps the most influential modern-day monetarist, said:

> *'There is perhaps no other empirical relation in economics that has been observed to recur so uniformly, under so wide a variety of circumstances, as the relation between substantial changes in the stock of money and in prices; the one is invariably linked with the other and in the same direction.'*

Friedman's modern **quantity theory of money** describes this relationship in terms of the following equation, or identity:

$$M \times V = P \times Y,$$

where M is the stock of money (changes in that stock being the money supply), V is the velocity of circulation (the number of times a unit of money is used in a given time period), P is the level of prices, and Y is real (inflation-adjusted) GDP.

The Conservative government of Margaret Thatcher embarked on a monetarist strategy for controlling inflation. It believed that by setting targets for the money supply, and keeping to them, it could control inflation. Unfortunately, this proved easier said than done.

At the same time as wanting to control the money supply, the Thatcher government abolished a number of controls on the economy which had been used by previous governments to regulate money and credit flows. These included **exchange controls**, abolished in October 1979, which opened the possibility for British banks to supply loans to their customers in Britain from overseas subsidiaries. The government also abolished (a) the so-called banking 'corset', properly called the supplementary special deposits scheme, which restricted the rate of growth of bank lending; and (b) **hire purchase controls**, which limited the amount individuals could borrow, usually for the purchase of cars and consumer durables.

The result of these actions was that the only weapon left for controlling the money supply was interest rates. These rates initially rose very sharply, to 17 per cent, but this proved to be of mixed success.

The government also fell victim to **Goodhart's Law**, invented by Professor Charles Goodhart, then a senior Bank of England official, later a member of the monetary policy committee. He said that any measure of the money supply targeted by the authorities automatically becomes distorted.

The Bank of England still produces figures for the growth in the money supply, mainly **M0** (M-zero), which consists largely of notes and coins, and **M4**, a far wider measure, which includes notes, coins, and all bank and building society deposits.

Monetarism was, however, abandoned in the 1980s and, following the 1990–92 experience of ERM membership, has now given way to the setting of inflation targets.

Bank of England independence and the inflation target

Prior to May 1997, when the Bank of England was granted operational independence, decisions on interest rates were taken by the chancellor of the exchequer, usually but not always in consultation with the Bank.

Surprise rate cut underlines City gloom

LARRY ELLIOTT and CHARLOTTE DENNY

The Bank of England delighted industry and stunned the City yesterday when it moved to prevent the economy sliding towards recession by cutting interest rates to their lowest level in almost 50 years.

In a move that will cut the cost of a £70,000 mortgage by £10 a month, the Bank cited the weakness of demand as it sliced 0.25 points off borrowing costs to 3.75%, a rate not seen since Winston Churchill was prime minister in 1955.

City economists, still taken aback by the first rate cut by the Bank in 15 months, were last night betting that the reduction would not be the last. Fear of war and the fragility of insurance companies following three years of relentless falls in share markets prompted some analysts to predict rates at 3.5% by the middle of the year.

In a statement announcing the decision, the Bank admitted that it had been over-optimistic in its expectations for growth in 2003 and 2004.

The surprise reduction in rates failed to cheer the markets, where there was concern that the decision pointed to the economy being in far worse shape than the chancellor Gordon Brown had admitted in a speech earlier this week.

Asked if the rate cut reflected desperation about the economy No 10 said: 'The PM believes we are in a better position than virtually any other country in facing the problems that the world economy now faces.'

This upbeat view was dismissed by Michael Howard, the shadow chancellor. 'This [decision] gives the lie to the complacency of the chancellor and the prime minister, and shows that there are serious causes for concern about the state of the economy,' he said last night.

Until recently, the Bank's nine-strong monetary policy committee had been resisting calls for lower rates amid concern that it could add fuel to the booming housing market. A majority of the committee were swayed by new weakness in manufacturing, the turmoil on the stock market, the poor state of the American and German economies, and tentative evidence that consumers are starting to tighten their belts.

'This is welcome news for business,' Ian McCafferty, chief economist at the CBI, said. 'The international economy remains fragile and there are signs that the UK economy is weakening.'

The Bank said it was not concerned by the recent rise in inflation above its 2.5% target, predicting that the recent increase in petrol prices would prove temporary and that house price inflation would start to come down. Its new forecasts for the economy, to be unveiled next week, are likely to add to growing scepticism about Mr Brown's ability to hit his forecasts for growth and public borrowing this year.

Ciarán Barr, chief UK economist at Deutsche Bank, said: 'The housing boom is the lesser of two evils; the bigger one is allowing the economy to slide into recession.'

Most of Britain's mortgage lenders were taken by surprise by the move, with most putting off a decision on their variable rate home loans until today at the earliest. The increasing number of people on tracker mortgages will see an immediate benefit.

The Guardian, 7 February 2003

For the period from the autumn of 1992 (sterling's expulsion from the ERM) to May 1997, the Bank's role was formalized. It was required to produce a quarterly **inflation report**, setting out its predictions for inflation, and there were regular monthly meetings between the chancellor and his officials and the Bank's governor and his staff. With Kenneth Clarke as chancellor and Eddie George as governor, these became known as 'the Ken and Eddie show'.

The minutes of these meetings were published, to show what advice the Bank had given, and how the Chancellor's decision had been arrived at. The Chancellor, while operating under a self-imposed inflation target of 1–4 per cent, was not under any obligation to accept the Bank's advice.

In the months leading up to the May 1997 election, Clarke consistently refused to raise interest rates – citing the strain on industry as a result of a rising pound – despite being urged to do so by both the Bank and his own Treasury officials. Critics said this demonstrated the shortcomings of a system in which interest rates were subject to political control, although subsequent evidence, and in particular a sharp slowdown in the economy, were seen by his supporters as vindicating Clarke.

After May 1997, with the Bank granted operational independence, monthly meetings to set interest rates continued, but this time only the Bank's monetary policy committee (MPC) took part – there was no political involvement.

The nine-member MPC consisted of five Bank officials – the governor, two deputy governors, its chief economist, and the director responsible for financial and money markets. Four more economists were appointed by the chancellor as 'outside' members of the MPC.

In 2003, the committee consisted of Mervyn King (governor), Rachel Lomax and Sir Andrew Large (deputy governors), Charles Bean (chief economist), Paul Tucker (executive director responsible for markets), Steve Nickell (a professor at the London School of Economics), Kate Barker (former CBI chief economic adviser), Marian Bell (ex City economist) and Richard Lambert (former editor of *The Financial Times*).

As in the 1992–97 period, the MPC's task now is to achieve an inflation target, this time of 2.5 per cent for underlying inflation excluding mortgage interest payments. In setting the target, the chancellor stressed that it was *symmetrical* – in other words that it was as bad to overshoot the target as it was to undershoot it. The governor is required to write a letter of explanation to the chancellor if inflation exceeds 3.5 per cent, or if it falls below 1.5 per cent. The minutes of the

MPC's deliberations are published two weeks after the meetings.

In order to arrive at its decisions, on which there is always a vote, the committee considers a wide range of evidence, including the following.

The economy's growth rate in relation to its long-run trend (2.5 per cent a year) and its position in the economic cycle

If the economy were growing significantly above trend and had done so for a number of years, so that spare capacity had been used up, the MPC would tend to raise interest rates.

Economists use the **output gap** to try to measure whether there is spare capacity in the economy. At the top of the economic cycle, the output gap is likely to be small, and continued strong growth will tend to be accompanied by higher inflation.

The labour market

Sharply falling unemployment is an indication that the economy is approaching capacity, and a rise in pay settlements would be interpreted by the MPC as a warning signal of inflation ahead.

Commodity prices

Commodity prices, such as those of oil and other raw materials, will tend to be influenced not by the strength of demand in Britain, but rather by world economic developments.

Movements in the exchange rate

A falling value of the pound will tend to raise import prices and add to inflation in Britain.

The recent inflation performance

Although interest rate decisions are forward-looking, they will be influenced by whether inflation is currently above or below the target.

Monetary growth

This is represented by the growth in the monetary aggregates, M0 and M4, and in bank lending, mortgage demand and consumer credit.

Asset prices

The faster asset prices are rising– such as house prices and the stock market – the more this is likely to be evidence of inflation in the system, or of a future rise in demand (because people can borrow and spend on the back of rising housing or stock market wealth).

To see how these factors influence the committee's decisions, the minutes are available on the Bank's website: www.bankofengland.co.uk

Is independence better?

Part of the reason why the Chancellor chose to give the Bank of England control of interest rates was to free himself for other aspects of economic policy, notably tax reform and improving the economy's long-run performance.

There is also, however, a strong belief, supported by research, which suggests that over the long-term independent central banks deliver low inflation, without sacrificing economic growth. A 1993 study by A. Alesina and L. Summers, *Central Bank Independence and Macroeconomic Performance: Some Comparative Evidence*, showed that countries which have had independent central banks for a long period, such as Germany and the USA, have performed better.

Other research has suggested that, in the early stages of bank independence, the trade-off between growth and inflation can be worse than before. An example is given by New Zealand, which made its central bank independent in 1989.

Figure 11 shows that both inflation and interest rates have been low in Britain since about 1993, but that this did not begin with Bank of England independence.

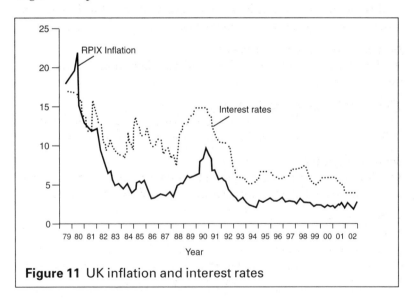

Figure 11 UK inflation and interest rates

How Bank of England independence compares with other countries

The Bank of England is operationally independent in that it operates monetary policy in order to achieve the inflation target (2.5 per cent) set for it by politicians. In other countries, central banks are left to judge for themselves what targets to achieve. The German Bundesbank, for example, operated a broad definition of price stability, and usually attempted to achieve it by setting targets for the money supply. The same is true for the Federal Reserve Board in the USA.

Another key difference concerns the decision-making committee of the Bank. In the USA, representatives from the regional federal reserve banks take part in the decisions. In the case of the European Central Bank, six council members are from the central directorate, but 12 are from the national central banks of the participating countries. Because there is no federal structure in Britain, interest rate decisions are taken centrally, a factor the Bank tries to compensate for by ensuring that reports from its regional agents affect its decisions.

Transparency is another important issue for central banks. The Bank of England is one of the most open and transparent central banks in the world, issuing the minutes of its decision-making meetings two weeks later and publishing a quarterly inflation report. The European Central Bank is less transparent, not publishing its minutes at all, for fear that the national central bank representatives who help make decisions on interest rates would come under undue pressure if it did so.

What will happen to monetary policy if the UK joins the euro?

By the time the Bank of England obtained operational independence it had been in existence for more than 300 years. Many economists, however, believe the current period of independence will be short-lived, because the UK government will decide over the next few years – following a public referendum – to join the European single currency.

Joining the euro would be different from previous currency arrangements that the UK has entered. During the period 1990–92, when the government was required to keep sterling within a specified range against other European currencies in the European exchange rate mechanism, the Bank could be instructed to keep interest rates at whatever level was needed to achieve that aim. In the end, even raising UK rates to 15 per cent in September 1992 was not enough to prevent the pound from crashing out of the ERM.

Joining the euro would be quite different. Not only would the pound's level against other European currencies be permanently fixed – and sterling itself would disappear as a separate currency – but interest rates would no longer be set in Britain. The governor of the Bank of England would simply become a voting member of the decision-making council of the European Central Bank (ECB).

At present there are 18 such members. If the UK and no other country joined the euro, the governor would have one vote among 19 on the ECB council. Thus, the two traditional weapons of monetary policy, interest rates and the exchange rate, would be determined at a European level, rather than a UK level.

This is why the Maastricht treaty emphasized convergence of inflation, interest rates and budget deficits – together with a prolonged period of exchange rate stability – as prerequisites for joining the single currency. Interest rates would still be set for Britain by an independent central bank, but it would now be the European Central Bank.

KEY WORDS

Monetary conditions	Liquidity preference schedule
Interest rates	Marginal propensity to
Exchange rate	consume
Money and credit	Transmission mechanism
Monetary tightening	Quantity theory of money
Monetary loosening	Exchange controls
Demand management	'Corset'
Exchange rate mechanism	Hire purchase controls
(ERM)	Goodhart's Law
Operational independence	M0, M4
Inflation target	Inflation report
Underlying inflation	Output gap
Monetary policy committee	Transparency
Demand for money	

Further reading

Balls, E., and O'Donnell, G., (eds) Chapters 3–6 in *Reforming Britain's Economic and Financial Policy*, Palgrave, 2002.

Bamford, C., and Grant, S., Chapter 3 in *The UK Economy in a Global Context*, Heinemann Educational, 2000.

Russell, M., and Heathfield, D., *Inflation and UK Monetary Policy*, 3rd edn., Heinemann Educational, 1999.

Smith, D., Chapter 11 in *Free Lunch*, Profile Books, 2003.

Useful website

Bank of England: www.bankofengland.co.uk/

Essay topics

1. The Monetary Policy Committee of the Bank of England has the explicit objective of setting interest rates to achieve the given target rate of inflation.

   (a) Explain the relationship between interest rates and the rate of inflation. [10 marks]

   (b) Discuss how effective UK monetary policy has been in allowing the government to achieve its macroeconomic objectives. [15 marks]

   [OCR, Q2, Paper 2887, January 2002]

2. (a) Explain how both fiscal and monetary policy can be used to influence the level of aggregate demand. [20 marks]

   (b) Should governments aim to influence aggregate demand, or should they concentrate on the supply-side of the economy? [30 marks]

   [AQA, Q3, Unit 6, Specimen Paper, 2000]

Data response question

Minutes of the Monetary Policy Committee, October 2001

Before turning to its immediate policy decision, the Committee discussed the world economy, aggregate demand and supply, the price of oil and inflation data.

The extent to which the terrorist attacks in the United States on 11 September would affect the United Kingdom economy was unclear. Early indications suggested a significant fall in retail sales in the week of the attacks, and there was evidence of only a partial recovery. Some sectors, such as air travel and tourism, had been hit especially hard. Share prices had fallen since 11 September, which would reduce households' wealth and would tend to dampen consumption. Investment (was likely to be reduced given the general increase in uncertainty. Many firms would face a rise in costs as the perceived need for security precautions increased and as insurance rates rose.

So there were elements of an adverse shock both to aggregate demand and to aggregate supply. The setback to demand would tend to (reduce inflationary pressure, while the effects of the supply shocks would tend to raise it.

The fall in the price of oil, to below $22 per barrel, from about $26.50 at the time of the Committee's last meeting, would reduce inflationary pressure if it were sustained. While political uncertainty in the Middle East (might otherwise have raised the oil price, the weaker outlook for world activity had so far constituted a stronger deflationary influence.

The RPIX had risen above its target level, although this was partially due to temporary factors. Inflation in the 12 months to August stood at 2.6 per cent, up from 2.2 per cent the previous month.   (25)

The Governor invited members to vote on the proposition that the Bank should reduce interest rates to 4.5 per cent. Eight members of the Committee voted in favour. One member voted against, preferring a reduction in rates to 4.25 per cent.

Adapted from *www.bankofengland.co.uk*, October 2001.

(a) Explain the role of the Monetary Policy Committee in achieving the government's macroeconomic objectives. [6 marks]
(b) (i) What is measured by changes in the RPI? [2 marks]
    (ii) Explain why the Monetary Policy Committee was asked to target the RPIX rather than the RPI. [4 marks]
(c) Using an aggregate demand and supply diagram, explain the sentence 'The setback to demand would tend to reduce inflationary pressure, while the effects of the supply shocks would tend to raise it' (lines 15–17). [6 marks]
(d) Using aggregate demand and supply analysis, assess to what extent a fall in the price of oil would be likely to 'reduce inflationary pressure' (line 16). [4 marks]
(e) Examine the likely effects of a recession in the United States on the UK economy. [8 marks]
[Edexcel, Q3, Unit 3, Paper 6353, June 2002]

Chapter Five

Modern full employment

'The government's strategy to help the unemployed into work has delivered structural improvements in the labour market. The resilience of the UK labour market in recent years has set the UK economy apart from most other industrialized countries, many of which have seen the rate of unemployment rise significantly over the past year or so. UK unemployment is now among the lowest among the G7 economies for the first time since the 1950s. Over the past five years long-term unemployment has fallen by over 300,000 – more than three quarters.'
Pre-Budget Report, HM Treasury, November 2002.

Measuring unemployment

Unemployment statistics are a source of intense debate. Traditionally, unemployment in Britain was measured by the **claimant count** – the number of people out of work and claiming benefit. Critics said that this represented only a partial measure of unemployment because it excluded many people who were out of work but not entitled to benefit, for example some married women wishing to return to work or excluded from benefit because of their husband's earnings.

On some estimates the difference between the two measures was large. The trade unions and some economists suggested true unemployment in Britain in 2002 and 2003 was three million, even when official figures showed under one million. To add to the confusion, in the 1980s there were regular changes in the method of calculating the figures, which tended to reduce the official total.

Despite this, the claimant count rose and fell sharply in the 1980s, only to repeat the pattern in the 1990s. Figure 12 shows this.

The Labour government elected in May 1997 responded to criticism of the claimant count by publishing a new monthly unemployment figure based on the **Labour Force Survey (LFS)** and in line with internationally-agreed **International Labour Office (ILO)** definitions.

This new measure, based on whether people were available for work, did not show unemployment above four million, but it did show a total nearly half a million higher than the claimant count. In early 2003, the claimant count stood at 0.9 million (3.1 per cent of the workforce) and the LFS measure was more than 1.5 million (5.1 per cent).

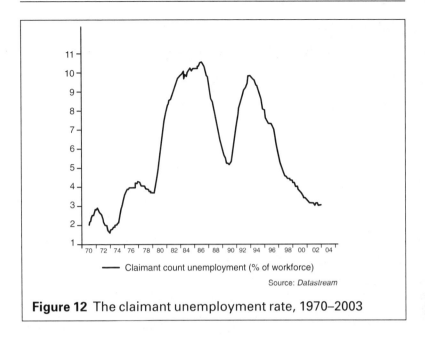

Figure 12 The claimant unemployment rate, 1970–2003

In 2002, LFS unemployment was 5.1 per cent in Britain, while unemployment rates on the comparable (ILO) measure were 6 per cent in the USA, 8.9 per cent in France, 8.5 per cent in Germany and 5.5 per cent in Japan. The EU average was 7.8 per cent.

Comparative figures for unemployment, and other economic data, are published by the Organization for Economic Co-operation and Development (OECD). Its website is at www.oecd.org.

Traditional full employment

Economists traditionally defined 'full' employment as being equivalent to an actual unemployment rate of 2–3 per cent, because in practice there will always be some unemployment, of various types:

- **frictional unemployment**, when people are temporarily out of work because they are moving between jobs
- **seasonal unemployment**, because some work depends on the weather and the time of year
- **structural unemployment**, caused by changes in the industrial structure of the economy, and the fact that it takes time to adapt the skills developed for one industry to another
- **regional unemployment**, because it is unlikely that labour market conditions will be the same in all parts of the country; for example,

the south-east of England could have full employment while there is still high unemployment in the north, as happened in the late 1980s.

Voluntary and involuntary unemployment

One of the central differences between the approaches of Keynesian economists and those favouring a monetarist or supply-side view is over the *causes* of unemployment.

- Keynesians typically argued that unemployment was usually **involuntary**, and explained by insufficient aggregate demand in the economy. The solution was thus for governments to boost demand.
- Monetarists or supply-siders believe most unemployment is **voluntary**, and caused by the fact that workers are not prepared to accept lower wages – they price themselves out of jobs.

Whatever happened to full employment?

After the very high unemployment of the inter-war years – the Great Depression – Britain and most other industrialized countries had two decades of virtually full employment in the 1950s and 60s. But from the early 1970s, full employment seemed no longer possible, and rising unemployment was accompanied by rising inflation. The economy experienced long periods of **stagflation** – slow growth or recession leading to high unemployment but accompanied by high inflation.

World economic conditions

World economic conditions were much more difficult. The two oil price shocks provoked by OPEC (Organization of Petroleum Exporting Countries) in 1973/74 and 1979/80 led to world recession. Britain experienced slower growth: just 2.25 per cent a year in the 1970s and 1.6 per cent during 1980–93.

Inflation

Inflation was no longer subdued. The oil price shocks, together with rising world commodity prices, produced an externally generated inflation stimulus.

Unemployment and inflation

The **unemployment/inflation trade-off** (see below) worsened – higher levels of unemployment were associated with higher inflation than in the past. This was due to the above factors, but also to (a) strengthened trade union power and militancy in the 1970s, and (b) structural problems, notably the decline in manufacturing employment. Manufacturing employment has declined from nine million in 1970 to under four million in 2003. Only by the 1990s was there sufficient growth in service-sector employment to compensate.

Policy emphasis
The policy emphasis shifted. Initially when unemployment rose, policymakers attempted to expand their economies to reduce it. In Britain this led to the Barber boom in 1972/73 under the Conservative government of Edward Heath, and the failed attempt by Denis Healey, Labour chancellor in 1974–79, to boost the economy in the wake of the first OPEC oil crisis. In 1976, Britain was forced to call on the assistance of the International Monetary Fund (IMF) and control of inflation became the new orthodoxy.

Demographic changes
Demographic changes were unhelpful. In particular the 'baby-boomers' of the 1960s entered the labour market in the late 1970s and the 1980s, expanding the available workforce and creating a serious problem of youth unemployment.

The international unemployment problem
Since the early 1970s, high unemployment has not only been a problem in Britain. In fact, compared with many other industrial countries the UK fared relatively well in the 1990s. As Figure 13 shows, unemployment throughout the industrialized world – the OECD is a grouping of nearly 30 industrial countries – rose sharply in the 1970s and 80s, eventually reaching more than 30 million.

In 1994 the OECD published its *Jobs Study*, analysing the reasons for high unemployment. It concluded that employment growth in North America, at 1.8 per cent a year since 1960, had been far stronger than in Europe, where it had been only 0.3 per cent.

The OECD said high unemployment, particularly in Europe, could not be blamed on new technology – the idea that people have been replaced by machines was not supported by the evidence. It also rejected the charge that unemployment in the industrialized countries was caused by imports from low-wage economies, or by increased global competition – so-called *globalization*. It recommended measures for countries to adopt to reduce unemployment. They were:

- setting macroeconomic policy in a way that keeps control of inflation but which takes advantage of any slack in the economy to achieve more rapid economic growth
- promoting the more widespread use of technology
- increasing working-time flexibility, for example by encouraging firms to open up more opportunities for part-time work

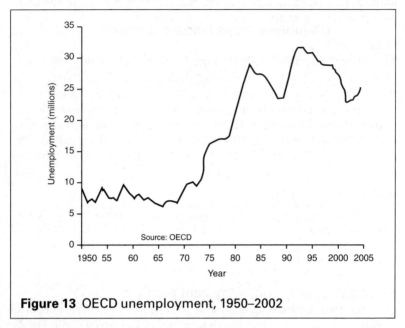

Figure 13 OECD unemployment, 1950–2002

- nurturing an 'entrepreneurial climate' by removing the obstacles to the setting-up and expansion of businesses – small businesses have been responsible for a substantial amount of job creation
- making wages more flexible, for example by allowing younger workers to be taken on at lower wages
- making it less onerous for companies to reduce staff – the more difficult it is to fire people, it was argued, the less willing firms will be to hire them in the first place
- using 'active' labour market policies, such as Britain's New Deal, to make the transition from welfare into work easier
- improving education and training systems in order to raise skill levels in the labour force – the evidence is that the unskilled have suffered most from rising unemployment
- reforming unemployment benefits, as well as other aspects of welfare – if welfare payments are too generous, there may be little incentive for workers to take on a job.

Since publishing the *Jobs Study*, the OECD has regularly published a scoreboard on the progress of countries towards achieving these aims. In general, the USA – which started in an advantageous position – has done well, as have the UK, Ireland and the Netherlands. Other countries in Europe have made less progress, including Germany, France and Italy.

UK jobless drops below one million

Unemployment in the UK has fallen below one million, its lowest level in more than 25 years. The number of people out-of-work and claiming benefits in February fell by 10,700 to 996,200. The figures are seen as a huge pre-election boost for the government.

Prime Minister Tony Blair greeted the figures, saying that 'full employment is within our grasp for the first time in a generation'. However, another measure to count unemployment, the so-called ILO labour force survey, is still well above that mark, falling by 81,000 to 1,535,000 – an unemployment rate of 5.2%. When the Labour party came into government, it said it preferred the ILO count – which is an internationally accepted measurement – over the claimant count.

Unemployment is falling in most Western countries, reaching a 30-year low in the United States, and slowly dropping in most economies of the European Union.

Workforce record
Another record was set for the number of people holding a job. The UK workforce is now 28.09m people strong, the highest level in UK history. The number of jobless last fell below one million in 1975, when the figure was 997,100 and the average weekly wage was £54, compared with £410 today.

The average inflation rate back then was 24.9%, compared with the current underlying rate of 1.8%. The number of people claiming the jobseekers' allowance had fallen steadily over the past few months, and economists did predict that the one million mark would be reached in early spring.

To mark the fall to six-figure unemployment, the government unveiled a package of new measures to bring people back into work. They include an extension of the flagship New Deal jobs scheme, which has so far helped 270,000 young people find employment.

The long-term unemployed and drug addicts are also expected to be targeted. Before the figures were published, John Monks, general secretary of the TUC, said: 'It is another step on the road to full employment and is in stark contrast to the 80s and 90s when full employment was regarded as an unacceptable dream.'

Source: www.news.bbc.co.uk, 14 March 2001

The unemployment/inflation trade-off – the Phillips curve

The **Phillips curve** owes its name to Professor A. W. Phillips, an engineer-turned economist who published an important paper in 1958 called 'The relationship between unemployment and the rate of change of **money wage rates** in the United Kingdom, 1861–1957'. Figure 14 shows a typical Phillips curve.

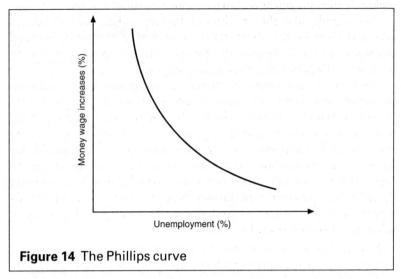

Figure 14 The Phillips curve

The price of labour (wages), he said, depends on the demand for labour. When unemployment was high, demand for labour would be weak and its price would stay low, implying small pay rises. But when unemployment was low, demand for labour would be strong, and firms would seek to outbid each other for scarce labour, pushing up pay.

There would thus be a trade-off between wages and unemployment. In addition, because wages were a key element in setting prices – many economists favoured a so-called **cost-push** explanation of inflation – there was an inverse relationship between inflation and unemployment.

The natural rate and the NAIRU

How can the Phillips curve explain the simultaneously rising unemployment and inflation of the 1970s and 80s? After all, the Phillips curve suggests a trade-off between the two.

Milton Friedman, the monetarist economist responsible for the modern quantity theory of money, provided an alternative approach, using the Phillips curve framework. He said there was a **natural rate of unemployment** for the economy, determined by factors such as:

- the efficiency of the labour market, including the mobility of labour and the extent of trade union **restrictive practices**
- the generosity or otherwise of unemployment benefits (the more generous, the higher the natural rate)
- education and training levels among the workforce.

If unemployment is below this natural rate, then demand for labour outstrips supply, and **real wages** (wages adjusted for inflation) are bid higher. If unemployment is above the natural rate, real wages fall.

This sounds like the traditional Phillips curve, and Friedman accepted that in the short term there was a trade-off between unemployment and the growth of wages. His key innovation was to focus on real wages rather than money wages.

Consider a situation in which a government has pushed unemployment below its natural rate by boosting the economy. Initially, real wages are pushed higher. But then adverse effects creep in. Inflation also rises, so eroding the initial rise in real wages. Workers notice what has happened and are determined not to get caught out again. Their expectations of inflation have changed. The change in expectations as a result of experience is rational behaviour: economists describe this as **rational expectations**. Next time they will want an even bigger increase in wages to compensate for an expected increase in inflation. This is illustrated in Figure 15.

Assume that we begin on the lower of the short-run Phillips curves. The government attempts to push unemployment below its natural rate and initially succeeds, at the expense of higher money wage increases. The impact of these higher money wage increases are, however, higher inflation, and the government is forced to act to slow the economy. The next time the government seeks to reduce unemployment below its natural rate, workers will be wise to the higher inflation that is likely to result and will demand higher money wage rises to compensate. The

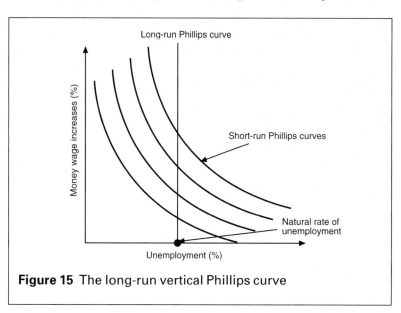

Figure 15 The long-run vertical Phillips curve

economy moves to a higher short-run Phillips curve, and so on, each time gravitating towards the natural rate of unemployment.

In the long run the Phillips curve is vertical – unemployment can be reduced below its natural rate only by supply-side measures, for example those which increase the flexibility of the labour market.

The non-accelerating inflation rate of unemployment (NAIRU)

Modern economists prefer to use the **NAIRU** in preference to the natural rate, because the latter somewhat callously implies there is something 'natural' about even very high levels of unemployment. In addition, while the natural rate came from monetarist thinking, the NAIRU is employed by all schools of economic thinking. Monetarists would place emphasis on supply-side factors, while Keynesians would say that demand factors can influence the level of the NAIRU.

To give an example of the latter, many economists believe that if governments and central banks run economic policy too tightly for a prolonged period, and push unemployment higher, this can increase the NAIRU. This is because, the longer that people are out of work, the more difficult they find it to get back in, because their skills become rusty and their confidence is eroded. *Prolonged unemployment can breed unemployment, and a rise in the NAIRU.* Some economists call this effect 'hysteresis'.

The NAIRU can be used to gauge policy. If policymakers allow unemployment to rise above the NAIRU, in the belief that this is necessary to control inflation, this is policy **overkill**. The opposite of trying to drive unemployment below the NAIRU is **underkill**.

The NAIRU is not easy to estimate. In the late 1990s, Britain's NAIRU was estimated to be 7 per cent on the ILO measure (see above), but unemployment fell below that without an acceleration in inflation.

Reducing the NAIRU – the Conservative approach

It is a desirable aim of policy to reduce the NAIRU, so that the economy can operate with a better unemployment/inflation trade-off. In the 1980s and for some of the 1990s, Conservative administrations under Margaret Thatcher and John Major placed much of their emphasis in reducing the NAIRU on trade union reform. Beginning in 1980, a series of parliamentary acts acted on the power of the unions by:

- restricting the 'closed shop' – the requirement that all employees of a particular firm must belong to a union
- making it more difficult for unions to start industrial action

- reducing the financial power of unions, and making them legally responsible for the financial consequences of their actions
- enhancing union democracy, both for the election of officials, and in the case of ballots for industrial action
- reducing the political role of the unions, by outlawing secondary action (when unions strike in support of workers in other organizations) and political action.

The union reforms coincided with a period of sharply declining union membership, from a peak of 13.3 million in 1979, to under eight million by the late 1990s. There was also a sharp decline in days lost owing to strikes and other forms of industrial action. Although the trade-off between unemployment and inflation did not improve in the 1980s, many economists believe these reforms were responsible for some of the improved trade-off in the 1990s.

Reducing the NAIRU – the Labour approach

While the Labour government elected in May 1997 left in place most of the union reforms it inherited, it introduced some policies that were seen to be reversing the trend – notably the **European social chapter** which increased workers' rights.

Labour also embarked on a new strategy, that of reducing the NAIRU by acting directly upon the supply of labour. The **New Deal**, financed by a £5 billion windfall tax on the privatized utility companies (electricity, water, gas, etc.), sought to bring excluded workers back into the workforce. Those aged between 18 and 24 years and unemployed for more than six months were offered one of four options – a job, training, a return to education, or a place on the government's environmental taskforce – with no 'fifth option' of remaining on benefit. Similar offers were made to unemployed people in other age groups out of work for more than two years, and to lone parents.

In essence, the New Deal offers the unemployed a subsidized return to work, in the hope that this will overcome the problem of 'unemployment breeding unemployment'.

The Labour government has also tried to increase the supply of labour, and reduce the NAIRU, by trying to overcome the **unemployment trap** caused by the operation of the benefits system. If available jobs are low-paid, and if people, particularly those with families, find that in taking up those jobs they are no better off than when they were on benefit, there is no incentive for them to take up work. The unemployment trap keeps them out of work.

The **working families' tax credit** (WFTC) later renamed the working tax credit, like the system of family credit it replaces, attempts to overcome this. People are given a pay 'top-up', courtesy of taxpayers, to give them an incentive to take up a low-paid job. The theory underlying it is that, once in work, they will tend to advance to better-paid jobs, and the tax credit they need will be reduced. The government calls this approach 'a hand-up rather than a handout'. It remains to be seen how big the effect will be. The Institute for Fiscal Studies suggested the WFTC would increase the supply of labour by between only 10 000 and 45 000 people.

The return of full employment?

By 2003 UK unemployment had fallen to just 3.1 per cent on the claimant count measure, well below levels regarded as possible even a few years earlier. Not only that but employment was, at nearly 28 million, at record levels, with nearly half of the employed workforce women. Was this the return of full employment? Not quite. On the internationally accepted measure based on the Labour Force Survey, unemployment was still more than 5 per cent, double the generally agreed full employment rate of 2–3 per cent.

According to the Treasury's own assessment, in the November 2002 Pre-Budget Report: 'The government's long-term goal is to ensure a higher proportion of people in work than ever before by 2010. Nevertheless, major challenges remain to reduce persistent economic inactivity and repeated periods of worklessness, and to raise employment in the most deprived local areas and among people from ethnic minorities.'

KEY WORDS

Claimant count	Money wage rates
Labour Force Survey	Cost-push
International Labour Office	Natural rate of unemployment
Frictional unemployment	Restrictive practices
Seasonal unemployment	Real wages
Structural unemployment	Rational expectations
Regional unemployment	NAIRU
Involuntary unemployment	Overkill
Voluntary unemployment	Underkill
Stagflation	European social chapter
Unemployment/inflation trade-off	New Deal
Phillips curve	Unemployment trap
	Working tax credit

Further reading

Balls, E., and O'Donnell, G., Chapter 2 in *Reforming Britain's Economic and Financial Policy*, Palgrave, 2002.

Bamford, C., and Grant, S., Chapter 2 in *The UK Economy in a Global Context*, Heinemann Educational, 2000.

Grant, S., and Vidler, C., AS Section 5 Unit 25 and A2 Section 3 Unit 18 in *Economics in Context*, Heinemann, 2000.

Hale, G., Chapter 5 in *Labour Markets*, Heinemann Educational, 2001.

Useful website

OECD: www.oecd.org/

Essay topics

1. Discuss the policies a government could use to reduce unemployment. [20 marks]
   [OCR, Qf, Paper 2883, January 2003]
2. (a) Explain the effects of unemployment. [10 marks]
   (b) Discuss whether it is possible for an economy to achieve full employment. [15 marks]

Data response question

Boom, boom ... bust: A tale of two economies

In 2001, for the first time in eight years, the annual change in real GDP of the United States (US) economy was negative. As the domestic US economy experienced a downturn, the number of people out of work (5 increased. The Federal Reserve, the US central bank, reacted to the decline in economic activity by cutting its interest rate to just 2% in October 2001, the lowest level for forty years.

In the United Kingdom (UK), the Monetary Policy Committee of the Bank of England responded by reducing its interest rate to 4%. High (10 levels of consumer spending, in particular, were helping to keep UK aggregate demand rising. It was feared that falling business confidence would have a negative effect on consumption and investment, and that aggregate supply, as well as aggregate demand, would be affected by the expected downturn. Compared to the US, the economic performance (15 of the UK was relatively strong at this time but the Bank was concerned that the UK economy would be adversely affected by the US recession.

Table A below shows the annual growth rate in real GDP and the average unemployment rate for the US and the UK economies from 1996 to 2001. Here, the US unemployment measure is based on the Labour (20

Force Survey approach, whereas the UK unemployment figure is based on the claimant count.

Table A Selected statistics on the US and UK economics, 1996–2001

	United States		United Kingdom	
	% change in real real GDP	% unemployment rate	% change in real GDP	% unemployment rate
1996	3.6	5.4	2.6	6.2
1997	4.4	5.0	3.5	5.5
1998	4.3	4.5	2.6	4.7
1999	4.2	4.2	2.3	4.3
2000	5.0	4.0	3.0	3.7
2001	−0.1[1]	4.6[1]	0.6[1]	3.5[1]

Note: [1]forecast
Source: *The World in 2002*, economist.com

(a) What is meant by the following economic terms as they appear in the text:
    (i) investment (line 13) [2 marks]
    (ii) aggregate supply (line 14) [2 marks]
    (iii) recession (line 17)? [2 marks]

(b) (i) What is meant by 'real GDP' (see Table A)? [2 marks]
    (ii) Use the data in Table A to compare what happened to real GDP in the US and the UK economies between 2000 and 2001. [2 marks]

(c) (i) Describe what is meant by the 'claimant count' measure of unemployment (line 22). [2 marks]
    (ii) To what extent is it possible to compare the unemployment rates between the US and UK economies as shown in Table A (see lines 18–22)? [2 marks]

(d) (i) Explain how changes in an economy's real GDP would usually be expected to affect its rate of unemployment. [4 marks]
    (ii) To what extent does the data relating to the UK economy (see Table A) support this relationship? [6 marks]

(e) In 2001, the US Federal Reserve cut interest rates on various occasions, reaching a forty year low in October (see lines 6–7).
    (i) What evidence is there in Table A to suggest why these interest rate cuts were made? [2 marks]

(ii) **Apart from a cut in interest rates,** explain **two** other measures that the US government could have used to stimulate aggregate demand. [6 marks]

(iii) Using an aggregate demand and aggregate supply diagram, analyse the effect of a **fall** in aggregate demand on an economy. [6 marks]

[OCR, Paper 2883, June 2002]

Chapter Six

Stability and economic growth

'The macroeconomic framework is designed to secure and maintain long-term stability. Large fluctuations in output, employment and inflation create uncertainty for businesses, consumers and the public sector, and can hold back the economy's long-term growth potential. Stability helps businesses, individuals and the government plan effectively for the long term, improving the quality and quantity of investment in physical and human capital and helping to raise productivity.'
Pre-Budget Report, HM Treasury, November 2002.

The business cycle

When economists talk of the business cycle, they are referring to the economy's tendency to display a regular pattern over time. This pattern can be simply stated. Beginning in the upswing or **recovery** phase, individuals and companies gradually grow more confident about their own and the economy's prospects, forgetting about the previous **recession**. They are prepared to borrow more, for spending and investment, and in doing so they push the economy's growth rate up – there is an increase in aggregate demand. Eventually, unchecked, the recovery turns into a **boom**.

The boom leads to higher inflation and, usually, balance of payments problems (strong growth in spending sucks in imports). The government responds by tightening fiscal policy, and the Bank of England responds by raising interest rates, in order to slow the economy, and the economy enters a **downturn** or recession, when it has slowed to the point at which policy can be relaxed again. This and the fact that, after a period of weak spending, companies and individuals need to spend to replace worn-out machinery and equipment, or household goods and cars, gives the next cyclical upturn.

This type of business cycle, with four or five years separating each cyclical **peak** or **trough,** has been identified during much of the post-war period. It is necessary, however, to refine it to cover modern experience.

There have been three serious recessions since 1973 (1974–75, 1980–81 and 1990–92) that were harsher than anything before in the post-war period. In the first two of those cases, external factors –

notably a sharp rise in world oil prices – played a major role. Prior to those recessions, economists believed **Keynesian demand management**, operating fiscal and monetary policy in a counter-cyclical way, had succeeded in dampening down the economy's cyclical variations.

The harsher post-1973 experience has led to a change in the definition of recession. Previously used to describe a period of declining growth (for which we now use *downturn* or *'growth recession'*) a recession is now defined as at least two quarters of falling GDP. **Depression** (or slump) is not the same as recession. A depression occurs when an economy reaches a cyclical trough *and remains there*. The last UK depression was in the 1920s and 30s. Japan since the early 1990s has experienced conditions close to those of a depression.

Figure 16 shows recent British cyclical experience, including the 'boom' of the late 1980s, the 'bust' of 1990–92, and the steadier growth since then.

Theories of the business cycle

Economists, long fascinated by the business cycle, have put forward different explanations of why it occurs. Indeed, they have identified

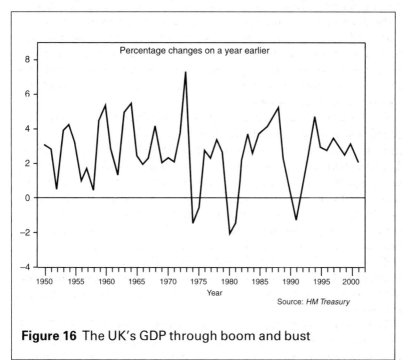

Figure 16 The UK's GDP through boom and bust

different kinds of cycle, including the 'long wave' thesis of Nikolai Kondratieff, a Russian economist, who believed that each upswing lasted for around 25 years, and was followed by a downswing of similar length.

In the 1970s, when the world economy embarked on weaker growth after two decades of strong expansion, many thought it marked the beginning of a Kondratieff down-wave. However, while unemployment has been higher since the early 1970s than before, and growth more erratic, it would be going too far to characterize it as a down-wave.

● Keynesian cycles

Staying with the more conventional business cycle, Keynesian economists emphasize the role of the **multiplier** and the **accelerator**. Producers respond to a small increase in demand by making a proportionately larger increase in investment in the machinery that makes it. *This is the acceleration principle.* The effect of this investment increase is to further boost demand throughout the economy through the *multiplier principle* (the initial stimulus comes from higher income and employment among the people making the machines).

Thus, an initial small demand increase is amplified in its impact, producing a build-up in economic growth, and eventually a boom. But when demand turns down, perhaps because of a policy tightening, accelerator effects are reversed – entrepreneurs cut investment in new plant and equipment disproportionately and multiplier effects operate in the opposite direction.

● Monetarist cycles

Monetarists believe that the business cycle is caused by variations in the rate of growth of money. An increase in the money supply initially leads people to spend more, because they feel better off. But when inflation rises, they realize that their money holdings (so-called 'real money balances') have been eroded in value. Thus, after the rise in spending, there is a period during which people rein back to rebuild their real money balances. Thus we have a spending cycle, and hence a business cycle.

Monetarists argue that the best way of ensuring that cyclical variations in economic activity are small is to maintain steady growth of the money supply.

● New classical cycles

New classical (neoclassical), or supply-side, economists believe that business cycles are caused by unanticipated **shocks**. These can be of the kind identified by Keynesians, an increase in demand leading to additional investment, or by monetarists, a money supply increase producing an initial increase in demand; or they can be the kind of 'external' shock such as a rise in world oil prices, which hit Britain in the 1970s.

New classical economists differ from the others because they believe there will always be such shocks, and that the business cycle cannot be avoided.

Traditional counter-cyclical policies

The demand management policies of the post-war period were driven by a Keynesian view of business cycles. If demand in the economy, both consumption and investment, is cyclical, then the policy response is clear: government itself has to compensate for such demand changes.

Thus, during a boom the government reins back on its own spending and other spending over which it has control – for example, investment by nationalized industries. It, or the central bank, increases interest rates. In a recession, the government 'primes the pump' by boosting its own investment and current spending, and interest rates are reduced.

Politicians used the analogy of driving a car. A 'little touch on the brake' would slow the economy, while a 'dab on the accelerator' would speed it up. Modern politicians are more humble about their ability to steer the economy – their favoured analogy is of piloting an oil tanker, with each change in direction taking some time to have an effect.

A scaled-down version of traditional counter-cyclical policies is that of allowing the economy's **automatic stabilizers** to operate. Tax revenues fall during a downturn and public expenditure tends to rise (notably because of higher payments of unemployment benefits). Rather than trying to increase tax rates or reduce other elements of public spending to offset these developments, the government allows these automatic stabilizers free rein. This means that even if the government is determined to rein back on public spending as a long-term aim, it does not do so in a recession for fear of making things worse.

Britain's cyclical experience

According to the Treasury, Britain has had more pronounced economic cycles than other industrialized countries – the economy has been more unstable. In 1998, it said:

> '*In each of the last two economic cycles, Britain's economic performance was poor compared with other G7 countries* [the

Group of Seven consists of the world's seven most important industrial economies — the USA, Japan, Germany, France, Britain, Italy and Canada]. *During this period, the UK had one of the highest average inflation rates and below-average growth. Fluctuations in output and inflation were higher than elsewhere, with growth ranging from minus 2 per cent to plus 5 per cent and inflation from 2 to 21 per cent. Interest rates and fiscal deficits were almost twice as volatile as those in France, Germany and the USA. All this damaged businesses' and consumers' ability to plan ahead effectively. It also contributed to Britain's poor productivity growth.'*

This more volatile record can be explained by a number of factors, and most notably errors in both monetary and fiscal policy. In November 1997, the Treasury published a paper 'Fiscal policy: lessons from the last economic cycle' – it is available on the Treasury's website (www.hm-treasury.gov.uk). This concluded that the Conservative government at the time underestimated the extent to which an improvement in the public finances – a shift from fiscal deficit to surplus – was due to cyclical factors. Thus, the government continued to cut taxes even as the economy boomed, believing that the strength of the public finances justified this approach. When the economy slowed markedly, the government boosted public spending to try to compensate, but the main effect of this, combined with a cyclical deterioration in the public finances, was to produce a record budget deficit (then measured by the public sector borrowing requirement) of £46 billion or 7 per cent of GDP, in the early 1990s.

The Treasury concluded that there were two main lessons from that experience:

- *Lesson 1:* Take a prudent approach. Adjust for the economic cycle and build in a margin for uncertainty.
- *Lesson 2:* Be open and transparent. Set stable fiscal rules and explain clearly fiscal policy decisions.

Fiscal policy errors are not the only explanation for Britain's greater volatility compared with other countries. Serious mistakes were also made in monetary policy. In the late 1980s boom, interest rates were cut to 7.5 per cent at the height of the boom in 1988, before being raised sharply to 15 per cent only 18 months later. According to the Treasury:

'The UK's relatively large cyclical behaviour reflects, in part, the consequences of policy mistakes as fiscal and monetary

policy decisions were taken without a clear framework and with changing objectives. Required corrective action was typically not forthcoming until it was too late, resulting in greater than necessary problems and excessive corrective action.' (Pre-Budget Report, November 1998)

Most of the increase in Britain's cyclical volatility, in addition, has come during the era of floating exchange rates. As an open economy which trades around 30 per cent of its GDP, and with a currency which is heavily traded, volatility in sterling has tended to transmit itself to the rest of the economy.

The Treasury believes the changes introduced since 1997 have made Britain less prone to 'boom and bust'. One indication of that was that during the world recession of 2001, when world trade growth came to a halt, the UK economy continued to grow. In its November 2002 Pre-Budget report, the Treasury said:

'The government's reforms to the macroeconomic framework are ensuring that the UK faces challenges in the global economy from a position of underlying strength, with low inflation and sound public finances. Historically low interest rates, a robust labour market, further gains in house prices and strong consumer confidence have underpinned solid growth in household consumption and allowed the UK to maintain stability despite an uncertain global recovery.'

Relatively stable GDP growth does not mean all parts of the economy are stable. One unusual feature of the economy from late 1999 onwards was a sustained fall in share prices – a 'bear' market – alongside very strong growth in house prices.

Does cyclical volatility hamper growth?

The Treasury, as noted above, believes that Britain's past record of having more pronounced cycles than other countries adversely affected economic growth. There are a number of reasons why this might be:

- Companies are cautious about committing too much investment, for fear of being caught out by a sharp downturn. Insufficient investment is a prime reason for Britain's lower GDP per head and poorer productivity performance compared with other countries.
- Companies may also be cautious about hiring and training staff, because they fear having to lay them off in the next downturn.
- The belief that inflation is always about to return means that workers negotiating pay are always looking to anticipate the next rise in prices, perhaps more than in other countries.

The Brown bear market

By GEORGE TREFGARNE

Gordon Brown is the longest serving Labour Chancellor and, until recently, he could claim to be the most successful. But he is now presiding over the most drastic collapse in the stock market for a generation and his reputation is going down with it. It is a long way from his blissful early years when he could take the markets for granted. Certainly, investors are worried about Iraq but that does not account for the FTSE 100 index vying with Germany for the title of the world's worst performing stock market this year.

So there must be something unique about Britain which is alarming investors. That something is Gordon Brown. This is a Brown bear market, made all the more sore-headed by his growling tax and spend programme. He is transferring huge amounts from the private sector, which generates wealth, to the public which consumes it. The market is buckling under the strain of carrying Mr Brown's weight. Sadly, nobody in the government has noticed.

Over the weekend, Tony Blair was still boasting about the economy's performance. 'Gordon has done a fantastic job,' he gushed. He may not hold that naive view for much longer. Shares ultimately trade on the health of future company profits, which are used to fund investors' dividends.

The falling market is clearly signalling a prolonged period of low or declining profits from UK plc and, by extension, a weakening of the financial foundations of Mr Blair's government. New Labour has turned out to be just as hostile to profits as Old Labour. Falling profits are partly caused by the downturn in the global economy. But in Britain, the government has exacerbated the situation by constantly increasing the burden of government.

According to figures from the Adam Smith Institute, taxes in Britain are rising faster than in any other European nation. In April, they will go up by the equivalent of 3p on income tax, raising £12 billion, as employer and employee National Insurance contributions are put up by one per cent each and allowances are frozen.

There have been more than 50 tax rises since Labour came to power. Apart from National Insurance, the nastiest ones are the windfall tax on utilities which raised £5 billion in the 1997 Budget, and the abolition of tax credits on dividends, which continues to raise £5 billion a year from pension funds. The simplest way to think of this is how long we must all work before we have paid the country's tax bill, which is marked by tax freedom day. Gabriel Stein, an economist at Lombard Street Research, says tax freedom day has gone from May 27 in 1997 to June 15 this year. Only then do we start working for ourselves.

The other cost weighing down business is more pernicious because it is hidden and hard to measure: regulation. Examples are the Employment Relations Act, which extended trade union rights, maternity leave and introduced the 48-hour week; the minimum wage; and red tape covering everything from fire safety to disabled rights.

The CBI reckons that the thousands of new regulations are costing £12 billion a year. Not only are they expensive to fulfil but also they have an "opportunity cost" as they waste time which could be more productively spent. Mr Brown is hoping low interest rates will get him out of trouble. But this is risky. Cheap borrowing has set off a house price boom and consumers are now deeply in the red from keeping the economy going. The Financial Services Authority believes over six million families are having trouble paying their monthly interest payments.

This points to Mr Brown's third mistake: he has got his arithmetic wrong. A black hole is appearing in his sums. Tax revenues cannot keep up with his spending. Sooner or later, he will either have to cut spending or increase taxes, or borrow more to fill the hole.

More government borrowing risks pushing up interest rates. But whatever the outcome, consumer debt has left the economy on a precipice, acutely vulnerable to a stumble in the housing market. For the 11 million with private pensions and the millions who own shares, the slump in stock markets is a very real issue. Perhaps if Messrs Brown and Blair had to save for their own pensions instead of relying on ones generously funded by the taxpayer, they would not be so complacent.

The Daily Telegraph, 28 January 2003

- Economic volatility encourages investors to seek safe havens for their money. In Britain, a relatively high proportion of investment has gone into housing – 'bricks and mortar' – at the expense of productive investment.

Professors Charles Bean and Nicholas Crafts, in a book *Economic Growth in Europe Since 1945* (Cambridge University Press), found that in Britain government policy could be criticized for its **'short-termism'** in seeking immediate results when inflation or unemployment rose, rather than pursuing a long-term strategy for economic growth. As such, it may have been a contributory factor in Britain's relative growth and productivity record. More important factors were, however, education and training and, at least until the Conservative reforms introduced under Margaret Thatcher, the poor industrial relations climate.

Government policies for stability

Tony Blair and Gordon Brown have pledged that there will be 'no return to boom and bust', and have introduced policies aimed at ensuring that the short-termism mentioned above will not shape economic policy.

In particular, Bank of England independence, with the Bank required to focus on achieving the official inflation target of 2.5 per cent, not only takes the politics out of interest rate decisions but is also intended to ensure that monetary policy is set in a medium-term context. It remains to be seen how successfully this will work. Although there is evidence that countries that have had independent central banks over a long period have less volatile economies (as well as generally lower inflation), it is not clear whether this is as a result of central bank independence or other factors. In the winter of 1998/99, when the economy was slowing sharply and the inflation threat was seen to be receding sharply, the Bank's monetary policy committee reduced interest rates quickly, just as a 'political' chancellor of the exchequer wishing to avert recession would have done. The Bank also cut interest rates sharply in the wake of the September 11, 2001 terrorist attacks on America.

The Labour government's other main innovation has been on fiscal policy. In the summer of 1998, the chancellor announced his first three-year public expenditure settlement for government departments, with spending to rise by 2.75 per cent a year in real terms. Subsequent settlements, the Comprehensive Spending Reviews of 2000 and 2002, signalled a more rapid rise in government spending. The idea, he said,

Budgetus prudens: Gordon Brown making a virtue of fiscal prudence

was to allow departments to plan properly for the future, but also, significantly, to keep a rein on any temptation he might have to relax spending further in response to short-term economic difficulties or pre-election political considerations.

The chancellor also published a **Code for Fiscal Stability**, a legally-binding framework based on five principles – transparency, stability, responsibility, fairness and efficiency – requiring the Treasury to report regularly to Parliament on developments affecting the public finances, and committing the government to two long-term fiscal rules.

- **The Golden Rule** means that over the economic cycle, the government will borrow only to finance investment, not current public spending (which must be financed out of taxation).
- **The Sustainable Investment Rule** requires the government to maintain net public sector debt, which in 2003 was 31 per cent of GDP, at a 'stable and prudent level' over the cycle.

The test for the new monetary and fiscal policy frameworks will be firstly, whether they can be kept to, and secondly, whether they continue to make a difference in terms of the UK's cyclical volatility, or whether they are outweighed by other factors.

Deindustrialization and the economic cycle

One feature of recent UK economic cycles is that the manufacturing sector has suffered disproportionately. Figure 17 shows this at work.

Soon after Margaret Thatcher took office in 1979, the 1980–81 recession hit manufacturing hard. It was caused by a combination of high interest rates and an overvalued exchange rate. Output dropped by a fifth, and a similar proportion of industrial capacity was scrapped. In the 1990–92 recession, caused by similar factors, manufacturing also fared worse than the rest of the economy even though that recession was dubbed the 'white collar recession'. In the late 1990s, as the economy as a whole skirted recession, manufacturing again suffered a prolonged decline in output, although this was less pronounced than in the two previous downturns. In 2002, manufacturing output fell by 4 per cent, its largest drop since 1991, while consumer spending rose by nearly 4 per cent.

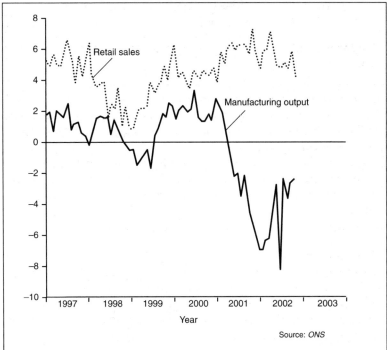

Source: *ONS*

Figure 17 Retail sales and manufacturing output (12 month % change)

Why does manufacturing suffer most? Most UK exports, about three-quarters, are of manufactured products. When a recession is caused by both high interest rates and a high exchange rate (and in a floating currency regime it is hard to have one without the other), industry is hit on both counts – the so-called 'double whammy'. High interest rates increase the cost of borrowing for manufacturers while the rise in sterling's external value makes it more difficult for firms to export. Domestic service-sector firms, on the other hand, suffer only from the high interest rates.

Why, then, do manufacturers not benefit when both interest rates and the pound falls? Sometimes they do.

In 1994, for example, manufacturing output rose strongly because interest rates fell; and the pound, following its 1992 departure from the European exchange rate mechanism, dropped to a highly competitive level at which it was easy for firms to export. In 1996–7, the pound rose again, and stayed high for several years, making life difficult for industry.

Cyclical variations in manufacturing output are, however, on top of another long-term trend, that of the declining importance of manufacturing (the 'secondary' sector, in favour of services (the 'tertiary' sector). Currently, manufacturing accounts for only just over 20 per cent of the UK economy, although many service-sector activities are also dependent on the manufacturing sector. In 1970, around nine million people were employed in manufacturing. This dropped to seven million by 1979, to five million after the 1980–81 recession, and to just over four million by the early 1990s.

At the time of writing, under four million people are employed in manufacturing. *Manufacturing has suffered from a higher level of cyclical volatility than the rest of the economy, while the process of deindustrialization means that the sector is in long-term relative decline.*

KEY WORDS

Recovery	Multiplier
Recession	Accelerator
Boom	Shocks
Downturn	Automatic stabilizers
Peak	Short-termism
Trough	Code for Fiscal Stability
Keynesian demand	The Golden Rule
management	The Sustainable Investment
Depression	Rule

Further reading

Balls, E., and O'Donnell, G., (eds), Chapter 2 in *Reforming Britain's Economic and Financial Policy*, Palgrave, 2002.

Bamford, C., and Grant, S., Chapter 7 in *The UK Economy in a Global Context*, Heinemann Educational, 2000.

Grant, S., Chapters 1–8 in *Economic Growth and Business Cycles*, Heinemann Educational, 1999.

Smith, D., *From Boom to Bust*, Penguin, 1993.

Useful website

HM Treasury: www.hm-treasury.gov.uk/

Essay topics

1. Discuss the potential costs and benefits of economic growth. [20 marks]

   [OCR, Qfii, Paper 2883, June 2001]

2. (a) Explain the phrase 'a fall in the growth rate of real GDP'. [5 marks]

   (b) Identify the likely effects of:

   (i) falling world oil prices on the level of real GDP in the United Kingdom. [6 marks]

   (ii) rapid economic growth on the environment in the United Kingdom. [4 marks]

   (c) Evaluate the use of supply-side policies as a means of raising the rate of economic growth. [15 marks]

   [Edexcel, Q2, Unit 3, Paper 6353, January 2002]

Data response question

Extract A

Technically no recession

1. Technically, our central forecast suggests that recession is avoided. A recession is defined by most economists as at least two successive quarters of negative growth. On this definition our forecast shows no recession, although the next four or five quarters are likely to see a rather weak growth.

2. This is just the technical definition for the economy as a whole. Many people and businesses will experience an actual recession next year. We will see a return to rising unemployment, projected by our model to increase by 160 000 in the next year.

3. Our model of the economy suggests that next year's growth rate is very sensitive to small changes in interest rates and exchange rates. So the downturn could easily turn into a recession if the Bank of England keeps interest rates too high for too long.
4. The Bank of England bases its interest rate decisions on its forecasts for inflation. Our model suggests that the 2.5% target for underlying inflation will if anything be undershot. It is, therefore, possible that interest rates could fall to their lowest levels since the 1950s and 60s.
5. However, the outlook for the economy also depends crucially on confidence. The amount of coverage given by the media to 'global meltdown' and the UK 'recession' raises a real risk that we could talk ourselves into an actual recession.

Adapted from *Lloyds Bank Economic Bulletin,* October 1998

Table B Central forecast

	Real GDP at market prices (Average growth %)	Household consumer spending (Average growth %)	Business invest- ment (Average growth %)	Retail price inflation (Average %)	Average earnings (Average growth %)	Unemploy- ment rate (Average %)	Bank base rate (Average %)
1997	3.5	4.4	8.8	3.1	4.5	5.5	6.3
1998	2.7	3.0	8.0	3.4	5.1	4.7	7.4
1999	0.8	1.8	−0.5	2.0	4.3	5.0	6.1
2000	2.5	2.4	1.1	2.0	4.6	5.0	6.1

Adapted from *Lloyds Bank Economic Bulletin,* October 1998

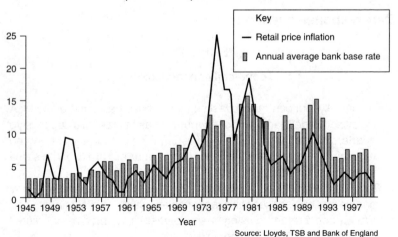

Source: Lloyds, TSB and Bank of England

Figure C 50 years of inflation and interest rates

(a) Apart from 'two successive quarters of negative growth' (**Extract A**, paragraph 1), identify and explain **one** important feature of a recession. [4 marks]

(b) Explain with likely examples, how it could happen that 'many people and businesses will experience an actual recession' (**Extract A**, paragraph 2) while there is no 'technical' recession. [6 marks]

(c) Use your knowledge of economics to explain how it might be possible to 'talk ourselves into an actual recession' (**Extract A**, paragraph 5). [10 marks]

(d) Discuss whether the best way for a government to achieve macroeconomic objectives is to establish an inflation target and then use interest rates to achieve that target. [30 marks]

[AQA, Q1, Unit 6, Specimen Paper, 2000]

Chapter Seven

Productivity and competition

*'Productivity is a key determinant of economic performance and living
standards. The government's long-term goal is that Britain will
achieve a faster rate of productivity growth than its main competitors,
closing the productivity gap. The Enterprise Act gives full
independence to the UK competition authorities and a new proactive
role for the Office of Fair Trading to keep markets under review,
strengthening the competition regime and seeking to bring down
barriers to enterprise.'*
Pre-Budget Report, HM Treasury, November 2002

What is productivity?

Productivity is usually measured as output per worker. When questions
were raised in the late 1990s over the future of Longbridge, the Rover
plant in Birmingham, it was pointed out that productivity at the factory
– 33 cars per worker per year – was significantly lower than at other
plants. The Nissan plant near Sunderland, perhaps the most efficient in
Europe, produced 100 cars per worker per year.

Since aggregate output across all industries and services is equal to
gross domestic product, productivity is a key determinant of **GDP per
capita**, or **living standards**. The raw figures on output per worker may
not, however, be that useful. The Longbridge workers may have looked
unproductive, but they were probably operating with outdated
machinery. In addition, while the Nissan cars were mainly assembled
using components bought in from outside, the Rover factory made
many of its engineering parts on-site. Thus, making a car was a more
involved process there and the lower output per worker could have
been expected. Nissan workers were still more productive than those at
Rover, but probably by not as much as the initial comparison
suggested.

There are other complications. A part-time worker cannot be
expected to produce as much in a week or a year as his or her full-time
counterpart. Thus, sometimes output per worker-*hour* is a better
measure of productivity.

Measuring output is another potential minefield. Rolls-Royce
workers produce fewer cars per year than their counterparts at mass
production factories, but this does not mean they are less productive.

Each car they produce is worth a lot more. It is necessary to calculate the **value added** in the production process to assess productivity more accurately.

Labour productivity is not, in addition, the only determinant of GDP per capita. A small, oil-rich state in the Middle East may have very high living standards but this reflects the good fortune of owning valuable mineral deposits, not high productivity.

As already mentioned, the amount of investment is also important. My productivity is raised because I am writing this on a modern computer rather than a manual typewriter. It is also possible to measure **capital productivity**, the amount of output produced for a given amount of investment.

Britain has tended to have lower labour productivity compared with other industrial countries, but higher capital productivity. If there were greater investment in the economy, labour productivity would be likely to rise, capital productivity to fall. Economists sometimes put these measures of productivity together to make what is called **total factor productivity**. The evidence is that on this measure the differences between countries is relatively small.

Why does Britain lag behind on productivity?

According to the Treasury, as Figure 18 shows, Britain suffers a serious productivity gap compared with other industrial countries. In particular, output per worker is about 40 per cent higher in the USA than in Britain, while France and Germany enjoy 20 and 10 per cent better productivity than Britain respectively.

Some of the reasons for higher productivity in other economies appear to be intrinsic to the economies concerned. The sheer size of the US economy means, for example, that companies can have longer

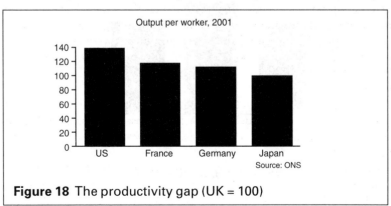

Figure 18 The productivity gap (UK = 100)

production runs and thus enjoy the benefits of **economies of scale**. A study in 1998 by McKinsey & Co., the international management consultants, found that one of the factors inhibiting productivity in Britain was that there were more planning constraints on businesses wishing to expand than in the US or France. In France, for example, it has been easier for new hypermarkets to open, while in the USA there is greater availability of land in general.

Most of the reasons for productivity differences are relatively straightforward. They include the following.

● **Levels of investment per worker**
Figure 19 shows that Britain's level of capital per worker (the amount of investment in machinery and equipment) is well below that of other industrial countries. According to the Treasury: 'The root of much of the productivity problem lies in a long history of under-investment.'

Not only do low levels of investment inhibit output per worker directly; they also limit the adoption of the latest, and most productive, techniques and technologies. Why has Britain had a relatively poor investment record?

Among the reasons identified by economists include:

● the City's 'short-termism', which has discouraged long-term investment by companies
● a banking sector which is also less supportive of investment by smaller firms than in other countries
● a relatively low level of savings as a proportion of GDP.

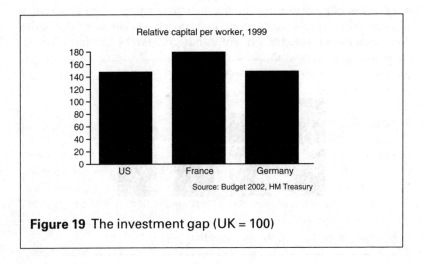

Figure 19 The investment gap (UK = 100)

Savings provide the funds for investment. Successive Chancellors have attempted to increase the level of savings by tax incentives such as Personal Equity Plans (PEPs), Tax Exempt Special Savings Accounts (Tessas), and now Individual Savings Accounts (ISAs).

● Innovation
British companies, while investing less than their international counterparts, are also relatively poor at **innovation** – putting new ideas and methods into practice. This, again, has been a long-term problem.

While British scientists have been good at inventing things, which are often first put to commercial use overseas, British companies have been relatively poor at taking them up. In 2000, UK businesses spent the equivalent of $400 per worker on research and development, compared with more than $600 for French firms, $800 for Germany companies and $1,100 for American businesses.

● Skills and education
Skills and education levels compare poorly with other countries. Britain has more early school-leavers than France and Germany. It is government policy for 50 per cent of young people to experience university by the time they are 30.

Workforce skills are also relatively poor. More than 35 per cent of the UK workforce has low skills, compared with fewer than 20 per cent in Germany and 10 per cent in the United States. Nearly 40 per cent of the US workforce has high skills, compared with 25 per cent in the UK.

● Macroeconomic instability
Britain's more volatile economic cycle, the greater tendency towards 'boom and bust' than in other countries, outlined in the previous chapter, hampered productivity by discouraging companies from investing for the long term in new equipment, new methods and the training of workers.

● Lack of competition
Productivity and **competitiveness** are closely linked. A country with high productivity levels will generally be competitive in relation to others – it will be able to sell its products in direct competition with them. Much of British industry, on this view, was inefficient and uncompetitive in the past because it operated within a sheltered home market. Once trade was opened up to imports, these inefficiencies were exposed.

Thus, the British motorcycle industry was wiped out in the 1970s and 80s by competition from cheaper and more reliable Japanese imports. The same thing appeared to be happening to Britain's car industry until foreign manufacturers decided to set up in Britain and produce for themselves.

The Treasury believes that greater competition in Britain is needed to enhance productivity. 'The government believes that businesses deliver world-class innovative performance only when they are exposed to tough, open and fair competition,' it says.

Policies to boost productivity

Productivity underlines the comment made at the very beginning of this book, that policies which affect the economy extend over a wide range of government activity. They include policies to encourage more savings and investment, perhaps through tax incentives, and additional public spending on education and training – Tony Blair's 'education, education, education'. Since taking office in 1997, the Labour government has increased education spending faster than GDP, a policy that continued in the 2002 Comprehensive Spending Review. It also spent the £5.2 billion 'windfall tax' on the privatized utilities on the New Deal and other programmes.

As with most policies aimed at achieving productivity improvements, the likelihood is that the benefits of improving education and training standards will show through only over the long term.

Other measures include:

- the encouragement of employee share ownership, because people are believed to be more productive when they have a stake in the business
- new incentives for businesses, particularly small and medium-sized firms, to spend more on R&D
- the stability-orientated framework for macroeconomic policy, aimed at ending 'boom and bust', discussed in the previous chapter.

There is also a powerful role, if lack of competition is a factor holding back productivity, for competition policy, as will be discussed below.

Is there a trade-off between productivity and employment?

We know that labour productivity is generally measured as output per person. It follows that there are two ways of increasing productivity. One is to raise the level of output for a given number of workers. The other is to produce the same output, but with fewer people.

In the 1980s, a productivity 'miracle' was claimed in Britain, because the growth of manufacturing productivity was more rapid than in

Productivity is the wrong target

BY DAVID SMITH

This government has chosen to target productivity, and the famous gap between Britain and competitor countries – 40% in the case of the United States, 20% to 30% relative to France and Germany. Britain has fallen behind and needs to catch up. Like motherhood and apple pie, few see anything offensive or even controversial about this proposition. The trouble is that productivity statistics are some of the least reliable we have. And international comparisons of productivity are worse than useless.

At the very basic level of comparing the output per worker of two very similar factories producing similar products, researchers have encountered extreme difficulties. The product range of the two factories is rarely identical, local market conditions vary hugely and other factors, not apparent on the surface, end up having a big impact.

Imagine then the problems of comparing different economies. Take, to begin with, the performance of the world's productivity leader, America. Can we take it for granted that US productivity is 40% above that in Britain and that, thanks to the new economy, the gap has if anything been widening in recent years? Actually, no.

According to Barry Bosworth and Jack Triplett, two economists at the Brookings Institution in Washington: 'The United States still has one of the world's best statistical systems. But it is evident that the system is faced with severe challenges in its efforts to keep up with the evolving nature of the economy. Much of the recent growth of economy has been in sectors that are poorly measured by the existing reporting system.'

It is hard enough, in other words, to compare productivity levels in the production of sophisticated manufactured products, where quality improvements can often explain away apparent differences. But this is as nothing when it comes to the services sector and e-commerce. How, for example, do you measure the productivity impact of automatic teller machines (ATMs), which have clearly revolutionised the banking industry?

Such difficulties exist everywhere, including in Britain. Sushil Wadhwani of the Bank of England's monetary policy committee is a productivity optimist, believing that the official data seriously understates recent UK performance. More serious than that is the fact that, as in America, the strongest recent growth in the economy has been in sectors where productivity is hardest to measure. It is a fact of life that, even though manufacturing represents only a fifth of the economy, it is still the area of the economy where we have the best handle on what is happening. Guessing service-sector productivity, despite its steady rise in economic importance, remains a nightmare for statisticians.

The big picture suggests that on international comparisons, Britain's probably low output per worker (labour productivity) is offset by high output per unit of investment (capital productivity). The gap in terms of what economists call total factor productivity is small, if it exists at all.

This does not mean we cannot do better. It is right to emphasise improvements in education and training and the transport infrastructure. We need a higher level of investment on a sustained basis. If all this flows out of a government obsession with the productivity gap no harm will have been done. But if we are waiting for the gap to close, and measuring progress every year, we will be disappointed.

Business Voice, April 2001

other countries. The components of this so-called miracle were interesting. In 1989, manufacturing output was barely higher than it was in 1979. Manufacturing employment had, however, fallen sharply – dropping from seven million to five million as a result of the 1980–81 recession, and falling further during the remainder of the 1980s.

The productivity improvements in the 1980s thus reflected lower direct employment in manufacturing. Some of this, in turn, occurred because firms engaged in outsourcing – where before they had employed catering, cleaning and maintenance staff, now they used contractors to perform such functions. Another reason for the improvement was the closure of inefficient firms. On the so-called 'batting average' argument, the closure of the least efficient factories will automatically result in a rise in average productivity levels.

Figure 20 shows that productivity and the rate of economic growth are closely related. In general, the faster the rate of GDP growth, the more rapid the rise in productivity.

It can be seen that there is a short-run trade-off between productivity and employment. In the long-run the most productive businesses and economies will be the most successful, and this will enable them to increase employment. *There is a limit to how much productivity improvements can be obtained by downsizing.*

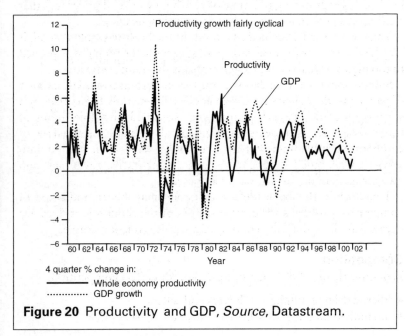

Figure 20 Productivity and GDP, *Source*, Datastream.

Productivity, competitiveness and the trade balance

Many economists would cite the gradual deterioration in Britain's trade balance as an indication of underlying problems in both productivity and competitiveness.

If productivity levels in the economy are relatively low, and wages quite high, then the competitiveness of British goods will suffer, in both home and export markets. Imports will undercut domestically produced goods, while exporters will lose market share overseas.

In the early 1980s, for the first time on a sustained peacetime basis since before the industrial revolution, imports of manufactured goods into the UK exceeded exports. This balance of trade in manufactures, once a source of strength for the UK economy, has continued in deficit since then. During the 1990s, Britain's overall deficit on trade in goods averaged about £13 billion a year, rising to £30 billion over the 2000–2002 period.

Is this proof of a problem of low productivity and a lack of competitiveness? Not necessarily.

When the UK first recorded a deficit on manufactured goods in modern times, in 1982, the country enjoyed a large surplus on trade in oil, thanks to North Sea production. One argument at the time was that the deficit on non-oil trade was a natural consequence of the surplus on oil trade, not least because one consequence of the UK's possession of huge oil reserves during that time of very high world oil prices was that sterling was pushed higher – it became a 'petrocurrency'.

Thus, what the UK gained as a result of the healthy surplus on oil, it may have lost on trade in non-oil goods, because the pound was pushed to too high a level to enable domestic firms to compete effectively.

Subsequently, while oil has become less important to the UK balance of payments, the deficit on trade in goods has generally been offset by a surplus on trade in services and other so-called 'invisible' items of trade. The UK, it appears, is a practical example of the law of **comparative advantage**. Greater resources have been shifted into services, where the UK appears to have a comparative advantage, and away from manufacturing, where it does not.

Thus, while the trade deficit in goods may be an indicator of competitive problems for certain sectors of the economy, it does not necessarily show that the economy as a whole is uncompetitive.

Competition

Economic theory shows that in conditions of **perfect competition**:

- there are large numbers of buyers and sellers
- no individual buyer or seller can affect the market price

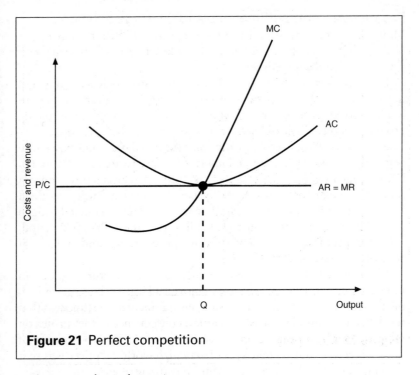

Figure 21 Perfect competition

- there is perfect information
- there are no long-run barriers to entry.

Figure 21 shows the standard long-run position for a firm operating in a perfectly competitive market. AC equals average cost, MC equals marginal cost, and the long-run average revenue (AR) and marginal revenue (MR) schedule is horizontal. Firms are price-takers. There are no supernormal profits. Now contrast that with the situation at the other end of the competitive spectrum – **monopoly**.

In contrast to the perfectly competitive firm, the monopolist is not a price-taker and faces a normal, downward-sloping demand schedule (AR in Figure 22). But, as the figure shows, the monopolist earns supernormal profits (the shaded rectangular area); and because there *are* barriers to entry, this situation persists in the long term. Under conditions of monopoly the price charged is higher, and the quantity produced lower, than in perfect competition.

Both perfect competition and pure monopoly are stylized examples. But even taking the contrast between the two, is it necessarily the case

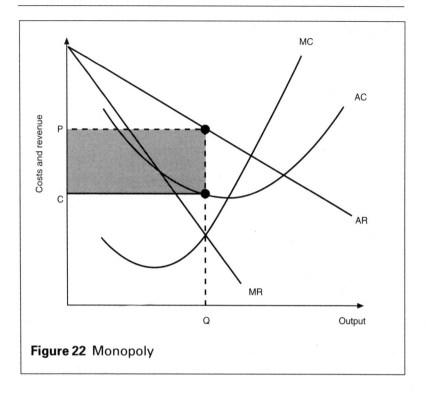

Figure 22 Monopoly

that monopolies are inefficient? After all, it may be that as a result of economies of scale the market will support only one producer.

Economists would argue, however, that this fact will be more than outweighed by other factors, notably:

- the lack of incentive for monopolists to invest and innovate
- the likelihood that, sheltered from competition, they will be inefficient.

Britain's former nationalized industries – British Rail, the National Coal Board, British Gas and the regional water and electricity boards – were inefficient for two reasons:

- they were protected monopolies
- they were not driven by the profit motive.

Privatization injected the latter, but only later was greater competition introduced.

Much of the criticism of privatization thus arose from the fact that, in the first few years after being privatized, the companies were allowed to continue making supernormal profits, or **monopoly economic rent**.

Contestable markets

In 1998, the government announced that it was strengthening competition policy in Britain with a new Competition Bill, giving new powers and a 20 per cent increase in resources to the **Office of Fair Trading (OFT)**. Under the new arrangements, the OFT was given the right to fine firms up to 10 per cent of their turnover for abusing their competitive positions.

This policy was further strengthened during 2002 with the passage of the Enterprise Act, whose provisions came into force in the spring of 2003. The Act gave, for the first time, full independence to the competition authorities – the OFT and the **Competition Commission** (previously the Monopolies and Mergers Commission). Under the new rules the OFT has the duty to keep all markets under review and to investigate those where it suspects monopoly behaviour. The Competition Commission makes and implements decisions without having to refer them to ministers.

Among the actions the competition authorities have taken in recent years include moves to bring greater competition to the professions, notably the legal profession, changes in the way the big banks provide and charge for small business services and moves (taken with the European Commission) to bring down the price of new cars in the UK.

One area of emphasis under the new approach is that the best way to ensure competition, a better deal for consumers and greater efficiency is to ensure **barriers to entry** come down, so that new firms can compete and prices fall.

Does competition increase productivity?

According to the Treasury, it does:

> '*A key part of the government's productivity strategy must be to ensure that robust competition in product markets thrives, over time driving productivity improvements towards world-class levels, and that there is a sufficiently strong competition regime to ensure that it does.*'

Interestingly, this was not always thought to be the case. One of the reasons for the strength of Japanese industry, for example, was traditionally thought to be that it had the benefit of a large, and protected, home market.

Japan makes an interesting case study. While its manufacturing sector, heavily engaged in export markets, was highly productive, the Japanese economy had low productivity across other, mainly domestic, sectors of the economy, including farming and service-sector activities such as retailing. These sectors mopped up much of the workforce, giving Japan low unemployment alongside industrial success.

Economists would always tend to regard competition as a good thing. Businessmen, however, may see it differently. While economists would expect the spur of greater competition to encourage firms to invest in productivity-enhancing equipment and methods, it is possible to envisage companies responding differently. They might see competition, and the threat of losing market share, as a reason to scale down investment plans. *Which of these two motivations dominates will determine whether a strategy to boost competition will raise productivity.*

KEY WORDS

Productivity	Comparative advantage
GDP per capita	Perfect competition
Living standards	Monopoly
Value added	Monopoly economic rent
Capital productivity	Office of Fair Trading
Total factor productivity	Contestable markets
Economies of scale	Competition Commission
Innovation	Restrictive Practices Court
Competitiveness	Barriers to entry

Further reading

Bamford, C., and Grant, S., Chapter 4 in *The UK Economy in a Global Context*, Heinemann Educational, 2000.

Cook, M., and Healey, N., Chapters 4–7 in *Supply Side Policies*, 4th edn., Heinemann Educational, 2001.

Munday, S., Chapters 2 and 3 in *Markets and Market Failure*, Heinemann Educational, 2000.

Smith, D., Chapter 3 in *Free Lunch*, Profile Books, 2003.

Useful website

DTI: www.dti.gov.uk/

Essay topics

1. (a) Explain what is meant by a contestable market. [10 marks]
   (b) Discuss whether competition increases productivity. [15 marks]

2. (a) Distinguish between production and productivity. [10 marks]
    (b) Evaluate two policies a government could introduce to increase productivity. [15 marks]

Data response question

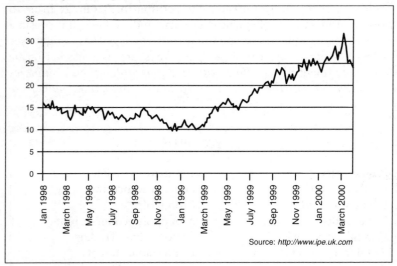

Figure A North Sea oil $ barrel

Extract A

Productivity alone 'will not offset high pound'

The rise of sterling against the euro was particularly worrying for manufacturers. The director-general of the British Chambers of Commerce yesterday warned the Chancellor of the Exchequer that productivity improvements could not be expected to offset the impact of the higher pound. (5)

The Chancellor had challenged firms to increase productivity faster than Britain's main competitors for the next ten years. He said that the government's "productivity push" would be stepped up in the coming year through reforms and incentives for the modernization of the capital, labour and product markets, but gave no details. (10)

The Chancellor echoed Tuesday's warning from Eddie George, Governor of the Bank of England, that there was no easy way of reducing the value of the pound without causing an increase in inflation.

Adapted from *The Financial Times,* 6 April 2000

Extract B

Bank of England Inflation Report February 2000

Oil and non-oil commodity prices have risen further, putting upward (5
pressure on producers' input costs. However, the appreciation of sterling
has continued to moderate the impact on UK inflation. An increase in the
degree of competition between firms may have added to downward
pressure on prices. The rate of inflation of retail goods has differed from
the rate of inflation for services. A decline in retail goods price inflation (10
has been offset by a rise in retail services price inflation. RPIX inflation
remains at 2.2%, below the government's 2.5% target.

Adapted from *The Bank of England Inflation Report,* February 2000

Table A European inflation rates

Country	Annual rate of inflation
Ireland	6.2%
Spain	3.0%
France	1.3%
Germany	1.5%
European Average	1.9%

Source: Adapted from *The Economist,* 20 May 2000

(a) (i) Explain the phrase 'productivity improvements' (Extract A, line 4). [2 marks]
  (ii) What is meant by 'RPIX inflation remains at 2.2%' (Extract B, line 12)? [2 marks]
(b) Explain how a fall in the value of the pound might raise the rate of inflation (Extract A, lines 12–13). [2 marks]
(c) Analyse the likely impact of a rise in oil prices on:
  (i) the rate of inflation [4 marks]
  (ii) the current account of the Balance of Payments [4 marks]
  (iii) the level of real output. [4 marks]
(d) With reference to the data in Table A, suggest **two** costs of a country's inflation being higher than its competitors. [4 marks]
(e) (i) Suggest **two** specific policies designed to achieve a 'productivity push' in the UK economy (Extract A, line 8). [2 marks]
  (ii) Evaluate the likely effectiveness of each of the policies you have suggested. [6 marks]
[Edexcel, Q4, Unit 3, Paper 6353, June 2001]

Chapter Eight

Devolution and regional policy

'*The creation of regional assemblies will signal the re-birth of political life across England. Our vision of regional governance is an opportunity for change and giving people the choice to make that change. This will be the conclusion of a political dream I have held for decades. Giving the regions their own democratic voice and the chance to improve their economic performance, delivering jobs, prosperity and better public services. This White Paper builds on the success of devolution to Scotland, Wales and Northern Ireland.*'
John Prescott, Deputy Prime Minister, launching the White Paper, Your Region – Your Choice, May 2002

Why regional policy?

Just as part of the aim of taxation policy is to achieve a more equitable distribution of income, so regional policy aims to bring about a more even spread of economic activity, and in particular employment between different regions. There is also, as the quote from John Prescott at the head of this chapter illustrates, a powerful political dimension to policy towards the regions. If large areas of the country believe they are being given a raw deal by Westminster, they will react against the incumbent government.

The UK is characterized by an uneven distribution of economic activity.

- The south-east of England (including London) covers only 11 per cent of the UK's land area but accounts for about 26 per cent of the population and generates 32 per cent of GDP. GDP per head in the South East is about 122 per cent of the national average. House prices are significantly higher in the southern regions.
- Five regions – the South East, the South West, East Anglia, the East Midlands and the West Midlands – together cover 38 per cent of the UK's land area but house 60 per cent of its population and are responsible for nearly 65 per cent of GDP.
- Typically, unemployment has been significantly higher in the north of England, Wales, Scotland and Northern Ireland than in those more southerly areas.

Figure 23 shows the way the UK is divided for the purpose of regional comparisons, and Table 3 shows the sharp regional differences

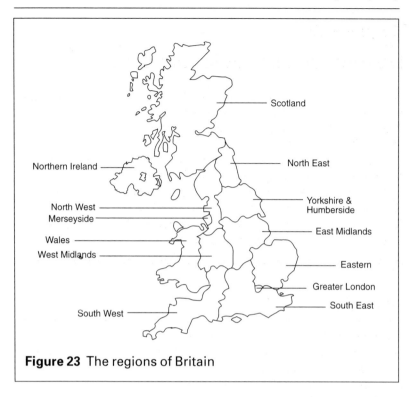

Figure 23 The regions of Britain

in GDP per head. GDP per head in London, for example, is 30 per cent above the national average, while GDP per head in Northern Ireland is more than 20 per cent below that average.

Regional policy grew up as essentially an element of employment policy (particularly in the post-1945 period) because wide variations in unemployment between regions would have made it difficult to achieve national full employment.

But regional policy is also linked to other objectives, including promoting growth and maintaining low inflation. Either goal is made more difficult if certain regions have an over-concentration of activity while others have a permanently under-used capacity.

The regional problem

Economists have identified three main types of regional economic problem:

- An **underdeveloped region** has never been a favoured location for industry, and has suffered from a decline in agriculture, the

Table 3 GDP per head and unemployment by region of the UK

	GDP per head UK = 100, 1999 data	Unemployment rate (%)
North East	77.3	6.5
North West and Merseyside	86.9	4.5
Yorkshire and Humberside	87.9	4.6
East Midlands	93.6	4.2
West Midlands	91.7	5.6
Eastern	116.4	4.1
London	130.0	6.6
South East	116.4	3.8
South West	90.8	3.7
Wales	80.5	4.8
Scotland	96.5	5.7
Northern Ireland	77.5	5.5
UK	100.0	5.0

The unemployment rate is the Labour Force Survey (LFS) measure for November 2002–January 2003.

Source: Regional Trends, ONS

traditional source of employment. Parts of West Wales, rural areas of Scotland and Devon and Cornwall could fit into this category.

- A **depressed region** once had a significant industrial base, but has suffered from the decline of key industries. Traditional industrial areas of the north of England and of Scotland, once reliant on steel, coal or shipbuilding, have at various times been depressed regions.

- A **congested region,** into which too much activity is concentrated, results in congestion costs, from overcrowded roads to wage pressures resulting from labour shortages and a decline in the quality of life arising from insufficient open spaces. The south-east of England and, for much of the post-war period, the West Midlands, were regarded as congested regions.

Two sets of factors determine which category a region is likely to fall into.

- The first are **locational,** where a region's location puts it at a disadvantage, because it is too far away from main markets, or because transport links are poor.

- The second are **structural,** where the structure of a region's economy acts as a disadvantage. Thus, when manufacturing industry experienced a third downturn in the space of two decades in the late 1990s, it was the West Midlands and northern regions of England which were most affected, the diversified regional economy of the South East, with its wide range of industries and services, least so.

Regional policy can be designed to act on both sets of factors. A way of alleviating locational problems, for example, would be to improve transport links, while a deliberate strategy of attracting new industries to an area can be used to compensate for structural problems.

The recent history of South Wales shows how regional policy has been brought to bear on both sets of problems. The extension of the M4 motorway and the building of the first Severn Bridge helped overcome the area's locational disadvantages; while new light industries, such as electronics, were given incentives to come to South Wales and replace declining coal and steel industries.

The rise of regional policy

In the 1950s and 60s, regional policy was regarded as an essential tool for governments wishing to maintain full employment.

The idea of the **regional multiplier,** whereby help for one region would spill over into additional demand in other regions, was popular. A policy which boosted output and cut unemployment in a region operating below capacity would be more likely to result in beneficial multiplier effects throughout the rest of the economy.

On the other hand, an increase in demand in an already congested region, perhaps through a national tax cut, could have an adverse effect, by creating inflationary pressures and the risk that the additional demand would merely result in a disproportionate rise in imports.

Regional policy operated in two broad ways:

- The first was through policies to encourage a shift of activity to depressed areas.
- The second was to provide people in those areas with an incentive to move to where the work was – to increase the **geographical mobility of labour.**

Though geographical mobility of labour is considered to be a good thing, as discussed in the next chapter, the first approach was favoured. By encouraging people in depressed areas to move to already congested regions, the former would risk losing their most talented and educated people, while the latter would become even more congested.

Within these two broad approaches, governments offered both the 'carrot' of incentives, and the 'stick' of preventing development in certain areas.

Examples of the former included **regional development grants** and other incentives for firms to locate in depressed areas. The latter included **industrial development certificates** and, for a period, **office development certificates**, used to prevent further development in congested areas such as the South East and the West Midlands.

In the area of encouraging workers to move to where the work was, the government provided assistance with transport costs and, for people moving from depressed areas, a weekly grant for a period to top-up their earnings.

Regional policy achieved some of its aims. Over the period 1945–81 the South East lost 1647 manufacturing establishments, and the West Midlands 334, a total of 1981 firms, while the rest of the country gained 1706. Successful though this shows regional policy to have been, it would have been more beneficial had the relocation occurred in service-sector employment. Another estimate, by the Department of Trade and Industry, suggested 784 000 jobs were created in assisted areas between 1960 and 1981 as a result of regional policy.

The fall of regional policy

Despite the apparent successes of regional policy outlined above, the Conservative government elected in 1979 embarked on a rundown of regional policy, for two main reasons.

- Firstly, it believed that businesses, and not the government, were best able to decide where they should locate, and that industrial development certificates and similar restrictions interfered with such decisions. The fear was that, instead of directing investment elsewhere in the country, it could prevent it altogether.
- Secondly, the Conservative government was committed to reducing public spending, and believed regional development grants and other government incentives were a wasteful use of public funds.

Within this approach, the government also identified regional problems as more localized than in the past. Instead of targeting entire regions, much smaller areas were selected. **Enterprise zones**, offering companies 100 per cent capital allowances on investment in the first year (they could offset all their investment against tax), exemption from local authority rates and development land tax, and freedom from certain government controls and bureaucracy, were created in 25 of these smaller areas during the 1980s.

Nor were all the areas selected for assistance in the traditionally depressed regions. When the government redrew the map of assisted areas in the early 1990s, not only did it significantly scale down the coverage of regional policy, but it also included parts of London (Park Royal and the Lea Valley), and the rest of the South East (Clacton, Dover, Folkestone, Hastings, the Isle of Wight and Sittingbourne) as eligible for assistance.

Devolution

In September 1997, referendums were held in Scotland and Wales on the establishment of a **Scottish Parliament** and a **Welsh Assembly**. Both were passed, although only narrowly in the case of Wales. The effect was to increase significantly the regional political and economic autonomy of Scotland and Wales.

In Scotland, following elections in May 1999, the 129-member Parliament, operating under a First Minister and an Executive of ministers, assumed powers for health, education, local government, housing, planning, tourism, police and fire services, economic development, financial support for industry, the law, and other matters. Westminster retained control of constitutional matters, defence, foreign affairs, most economic and financial matters, social security, competition and consumer protection policy, and other 'national' issues.

Significantly, the Scottish Parliament was given the power to vary the basic rate of income tax – either up or down – by up to three pence in the pound, using the proceeds to increase public spending in Scotland, in the case of a rise in tax, or cutting the rate of tax to cut spending.

In the case of Wales, the Assembly – also operating under a First Minister and Executive – assumed responsibility for the £9 billion annual Welsh Office budget and thus took responsibility for health, education, environmental matters, and the other broad policy areas similarly devolved to the Scottish Parliament. Unlike in Scotland, however, the Assembly has no powers to vary income tax.

Regional assemblies

Devolution led to demand from English regions for greater autonomy. This included the election of a London mayor and assembly, as well as elected mayors in other cities. In May 2002 the Labour government published a regional White Paper, called Your Region – Your Choice. It proposed further changes on top of the existing Regional Development Agencies (RDAs). The RDAs, described as 'economic powerhouses' by the government, have the task of developing economic strategies for each region, and of attracting investment.

Tories prepare to defy leader on tartan tax

BY DAVID SCOTT

Scottish Tories appear set to go against the tax-cutting policies of Iain Duncan Smith by refusing to pledge reductions under the parliament's 'tartan tax' variation powers.

Annabel Goldie, the deputy leader of the Scottish Conservatives, said in a radio interview aired today that attempts to lower taxes immediately would be dangerous, premature and feckless.

The Scottish Tories could promise tax cuts for Scots by making use of the parliament's tax-varying powers that allow an increase or a decrease in tax of up to 3p in the pound.

However, Ms Goldie made it clear in an interview with Radio Forth that it would be "dangerous to tamper with the tax-varying powers of the parliament".

Until now, the Scottish Tories have not made any commitment over the use of the so-called tartan tax, but Ms Goldie's comments clearly suggest there will be no commitment to lower taxes in the party's election manifesto for the May elections.

Her remarks will be seen as going against the view of Mr Duncan Smith. While there is apparent confusion in the UK Tory ranks about tax cuts, Mr Duncan Smith said last month that an incoming Conservative government would be a 'lower tax, lower regulating party than the outgoing Labour Party'.

The Scottish Tory policy on taxation would also mean the party would be un-able to present an alternative to the policies of other parties on the key issue of taxation.

Jack McConnell has already ruled out the use of the varying power to increase taxes in the next parliament. The SNP and the Liberal Democrats have yet to make a final decision, but are expected to argue that increasing taxes would be unnecessary.

Ms Goldie, who is also the Tories' economic spokesman and a list MSP for West of Scotland, said in the interview that, naturally, the Conservatives would always be interested in creating an environment for business which was as helpful as possible.

She went on: 'What we have to consider is that, if we do contemplate in any way cutting taxes, we would have to look at public expenditure also and try to keep the economy stable.'

The MSP acknowledged there were always options to be considered in relation to the economy. But she added: 'What the Tory party in Scotland is very clear about is that it would be premature at this stage to talk about interfering with the tax-varying powers.'

In his comments last month, Mr Duncan Smith said a Tory government would run a lower tax regime than Labour by increasing the involvement of the private and voluntary sectors in public services. He stressed this would be his party's policy.

The Scotsman, 10 January 2003

In the May 2002 White Paper, regions were given the opportunity to establish elected assemblies, the aims of which would be to decentralize power from central government, give regions more freedom and flexibility, increasing accountability and promoting sustainable development. It remains to be seen how many regions will take up the opportunity.

Despite these changes, it does not appear that regional policy will revert to its former levels. The new approach is based on regional 'self-help' rather than large-scale redistribution from the centre. In June 2002, in his Mansion House speech in the City of London, Gordon Brown, the chancellor of the exchequer, said the government would not try to prevent development in the South East in order to boost other regions.

The economics of independence

In the case of Scotland, if not Wales, many observers see devolution as a stepping-stone towards full independence, as is the policy aim of the Scottish National Party (SNP). An independent Scotland, it is argued, could run its own economic affairs, and adopt a separate currency or join the euro ahead of any decision to do so by the British government.

Scotland, with a population of five million, is certainly not too small an economic unit to prosper within the EU – there are smaller EU member states. One central argument, however, is the extent to which Scotland is currently supported by the rest of the UK.

Table 4 Identifiable government expenditure per head, 2000–01 (£)

North West	4888
North East	5148
Yorkshire and Humberside	4669
East Midlands	4280
West Midlands	4491
South West	4312
Eastern	4142
London	5067
South East	4000
England	4529
Scotland	5558
Wales	5302
Northern Ireland	6424
United Kingdom	4709

Source: HM Treasury Public Expenditure Statistics (www.hm-treasury.gov.uk)

Table 4 shows Treasury data for government expenditure per head by region. Scotland has government expenditure per head of over £1000 more than England, and over £1500 more than the lowest English region, the South East (although note that London is high because of the concentration of civil service activity in the capital). Wales is also well above the English average, Northern Ireland even more so, partly because of high levels of security expenditure.

Scotland has higher government expenditure per head because, for example, the population is spread out over a wide area, making the delivery of public services more expensive. The argument this provides *against* devolution is that, if these costs had to be financed by Scottish taxpayers alone, the tax burden in Scotland would rise sharply relative to the rest of the UK, providing an incentive for businesses and individuals to relocate to England.

This argument is, however, strongly challenged by the SNP. It suggests that, far from being subsidized by the rest of the UK, Scotland had a budget surplus with the rest of the UK of £91 billion over the period 1979–94. The figure was arrived at largely by allocating 90 per cent of North Sea oil revenues to Scotland. The argument over the costs and benefits of independence are likely to feature strongly in the policy debate in the coming years.

Three reports published during the run-up to the May 1999 elections to the Scottish Parliament, by the David Hume Institute, the Pieda economic consultancy and the Centre for Economics and Business Research, concluded that an independent Scotland would face a 'negative dowry' – a gap between public spending and taxation – arising from the loss of the UK subsidy (i.e. the fact that public expenditure per head is higher in Scotland). This would require, they said, either a reduction in public spending or higher taxation.

All three reports concluded, however, that the success of an independent Scotland over the longer-term would depend on the ability of politicians to adopt supply-side economic policies that were friendly towards the creation of new businesses and jobs. Within the UK, Scotland's modern record on both counts has been mixed.

KEY WORDS

Underdeveloped region
Depressed region
Congested region
Locational factors
Structural factors
Regional multiplier
Geographical mobility of
    labour
Regional development grants

Industrial development
    certificates
Office development certificates
Enterprise zones
Scottish Parliament
Welsh Assembly
Regional Development
    Agencies
Single Regeneration Budget

Further reading

Grant, S., and Vidler, C., A2 Section 2 Unit 8 in *Economics in Context*, Heinemann Educational, 2001.

Griffiths, A., and Wall, S., Chapter 21 in *Applied Economics*, 10th edn., Addison-Wesley Longman, 2003.

Hill, B., Chapter 5 in *The European Union*, 4th edn., Heinemann Educational, 2001.

Smith, D., *North and South*, Penguin, 1994.

Essay topics

1. (a) Why are some regions in the UK poorer than others? [10 marks]
   (b) Assess the risks of the UK becoming one of the poor regions of the European Union. [15 marks]
2. Discuss the implications for the UK economy of Scottish and Welsh devolution. [25 marks]

Useful websites

Scottish Office: www.scotland.gov.uk/
Scottish National Party: www.snp.org.uk/

Data response question

Table A Scotland: general expenditure and revenues in
Scotland 1999–2000

Revenues	£ Millions	
Income tax (after tax credits	6,500	
VAT	4,900	
Social security contributions (NICs)	4,800	
Local authority revenues	2,700	
Corporation taxes (excluding North Sea receipts)	2,900	
Other revenue (e.g. air passenger duty)	8,000	
Total		**29,800**
SPENDING		
Education	4,418	
Health and personal social services	6,518	
Roads and transport	924	
Housing	458	
Other environmental services	963	
Law and order, and protective service	1,545	
Trade, industry, energy and employment	1,076	
Agriculture, fisheries, food and forestry	1,050	
Culture, media and sport	453	
Social security	9,611	
Defence	1,936	
Overseas services and aid	292	
Miscellaneous spending	953	
Debt interest etc	4,000	
Adjustment for EU transactions, and reconcillation	–320	
Total		**33,877**
Balance		**–4077 (deficit)**

North sea oil revenue		Balance with oil revenue
With oil price at $15 a barrel	1,600	–2,477 (deficit)
With oil price at $25 a barrel	4,200	123 (surplus)

Based on Government Expenditure and Revenues in Scotland, 1999–2000,
Scottish Executive/*Times* estimates'

Scotland's struggle to balance the books

But we do not really need certainty over the numbers to answer the
question, 'could Scotland feasibly go it alone?'

The answer clearly must be that it could. Even with a deficit of 3 per cent of GDP, Scotland would be as capable as any other small country of financing its borrowing by issuing government bonds, though prudence might require some tax rises or spending cuts, too.

It would be bizarre to reach any other conclusion. As a nation of five million people with a GDP per head close to that of the UK as a whole, Scotland can readily stand among the ranks of wealthy small countries such as the Irish Republic and Denmark. It is hard to think of reasons why they should be capable of an independent existence while Scotland would be terminally handicapped.

Of course, none of this means that Scotland would be more prosperous alone than in the Union. Opponents of independence might sensibly argue that the economy of an independent Scotland would be peculiarly vulnerable to the caprices of a volatile oil market.

Freed from its constitutional ties to the UK, just how independent could Scotland truly be?

Opec would be just one powerful outside influence among many, of which the most powerful would probably remain England. Having dissolved its political union, Scotland's economy would remain intimately bound up with that of its larger, wealthier neighbour, in myriad ways. And while independence would probably mean Scotland quickly joining the euro, it would merely have traded interest rates by a "remote" Bank of England in London for rates set still further away, by an even less accountable institution in Frankfurt.

An independent Scotland might be apart from England. But it would be far from going it alone in a world where no country can any longer be an island.   *The Times*, 20 August 2002, Gary Duncan

(a) (i) Using Table 1, explain whether Scotland had a budget deficit in 1999–2000. [4 marks]

  (ii) Describe two ways in which a budget deficit could be financed. [4 marks]

(b) Using an aggregate demand and aggregate supply diagram, analyse the effect of a rise in government expenditure on the Scottish economy. [8 marks]

(c) (i) Why is Scotland 'particularly vulnerable to the caprices of a volatile oil market' (see the extract from Times above). [5 marks]

  (ii) Why is the oil market a volatile one? [6 marks]

(d) Assess two advantages and two disadvantages Scotland may experience as a result of joining the euro. [8 marks]

(e) Discuss whether an independent Scotland would be more prosperous than a devolved Scotland. [10 marks]

Chapter Nine

Britain, Europe and the euro

'In principle, the government is in favour of UK membership of the singe currency; in practice the economic conditions must be right. The determining factor is the national economic interest and whether the economic case for joining is clear and unambiguous. The government has set out five economic tests which must be met before any decision to join can be made ...If a decision to recommend joining is taken by the government, it will be put to a vote in Parliament and then to a referendum of the British people.'
Pre-Budget Report, HM Treasury, November 2002.

The UK and the European Union

The history of the modern **European Union** (EU) dates back to the early 1950s when six European countries – France, Germany, Belgium, the Netherlands, Luxembourg and Italy – signed the Treaty of Paris of 1951, establishing the **European Coal and Steel Community** (ECSC), which provided for co-operation in these industries. Britain was invited to take part in the initial discussions but declined to join.

Six years later, in 1957, the **Treaty of Rome** was signed by the Six, this time bringing into being the **European Economic Community** (EEC) – another treaty was signed at the same time establishing Euratom, the European Atomic Energy Community. Britain, again, did not join, preferring instead to forge a separate free trade area, the **European Free Trade Association** (EFTA), along with Austria, Denmark, Norway, Portugal, Sweden and Switzerland, in 1960.

Within the EEC, the **Common Agricultural Policy** (CAP), providing a wide-ranging, and costly, system of price support for farm produce was introduced in 1962. By 1968, after progressive reductions in internal tariffs, and the convergence by the Six around a **common external tariff**, the EEC had become a **customs union**.

The UK first applied for membership of the EEC in 1961 but was rejected on two occasions, in 1963 and 1967, largely because of the opposition of the then French president, General de Gaulle. Britain finally joined, on 1 January 1973, along with Denmark and Ireland.

Further enlargements took place in 1981 (Greece), 1986 (Spain and Portugal), and 1995 (Austria, Finland and Sweden), making 15 members in all.

During the 1980s, with Margaret Thatcher as British prime minister, much European Community business was taken up with the issue of Britain's contribution to the budget – she successfully won a rebate at Fontainebleau in 1984. Britain was also influential in pushing for the **Single European Act** of 1987, which established the European **single market** at the beginning of 1993, and thus Europe started on the road to becoming a true **common market**.

Britain was less enthusiastic about the **Treaty on European Union**, agreed at Maastricht in December 1991, which provided for **European economic and monetary union** (EMU) as well as closer co-operation on other matters, notably social policy, including workers' rights. John Major, as prime minister, secured the right of the UK to opt-in to both EMU and the so-called **social protocol** on workers' rights at a time of the government's choosing. The Labour government elected in 1997 opted in to many of the provisions of the social protocol, for example the working time directive, which limited the working week to 48 hours. Under the Maastricht treaty, the European Communities (the combined name for the EEC, ECSC and Euratom) became the European Union.

Customs unions and common markets

The EEC was popularly known as the Common Market from its inception in the 1950s. It was, however, more correctly described as a customs union, defined as an area with a common external tariff (i.e. goods entering the area would face the same tariff or other restriction no matter which country they entered).

The second requirement of a customs union is that there be no internal tariffs on trade. A customs union was thus achieved for the original six EEC members by the late 1960s.

A common market is more ambitious. It means a free market within the area in goods, services, capital and people – no restrictions on the ability of individuals to live and work elsewhere in the area. The move to establish a true common market in Europe began with the Single European Act.

Is a customs union and/or a common market a good thing? Both represent a *limited* free trade area, rather than universal free trade. Economists define two effects from the creation of a customs union and its evolution into a common market:

- The first is **trade creation** – lowering internal trade barriers within the EU has led to increased trade between member countries.
- The second is **trade diversion** – the preferential treatment accorded to trade between member countries diverts trade away from other countries.

The common external tariff, in other words, can be expected to result in a fall-off in imports from outside the EU. If this tariff is set at a high level, then it is possible that, for consumers, the negative effects of trade diversion could outweigh the positive impact of trade creation. Economists agree that universal free trade is better than limited free

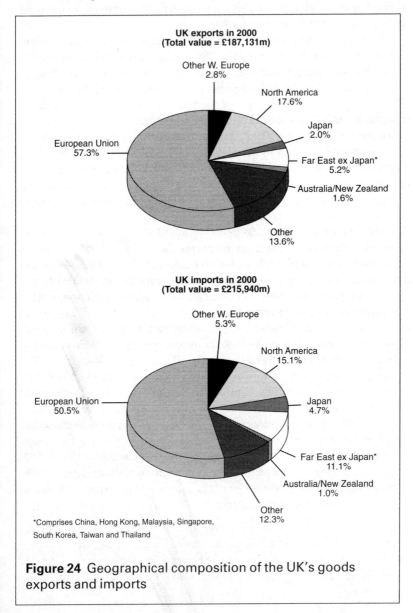

Figure 24 Geographical composition of the UK's goods exports and imports

trade. The latter is known as a **second-best solution**.

The effects of both trade creation and trade diversion can be seen clearly in the statistics. Nearly 60 per cent of the external trade of members of the EU is, on average, with other member countries, a figure which rises to more than 75 per cent in the case of Belgium and Luxembourg. In 1958 about a quarter of Britain's external trade was with the other 14 members of the current EU. Trade with the Commonwealth and with the USA was, in overall terms, much more important. By 1980, after membership, this had risen to more than 40 per cent. The recent position, with about 55 per cent of export and import trade with other EU countries, is shown in Figure 24.

European economic and monetary union

From the very start of the post-war process of European integration, indeed on occasions in more distant history, politicians have seen the creation of a single currency for Europe – of economic and monetary union – as a central goal. While countries can enter and leave customs unions, common markets and other such arrangements, a single currency was always regarded as a binding form of integration, which would permanently unite member states, although not everybody agrees that the single currency will achieve this.

In 1969, at a summit in The Hague, leaders of the six EEC countries agreed to adopt the goal of achieving monetary union. In 1970, the **Werner committee**, under the chairmanship of Pierre Werner, the Luxembourg Prime Minister, proposed a timetable for achieving monetary union by 1980 and this was adopted by European leaders. However, events in international financial markets, including the collapse of the post-war **Bretton Woods** system of fixed-but-adjustable exchange rates, and the economic crisis caused by the first Organization of Petroleum Exporting Countries' (OPEC) oil price hike, led to this timetable being abandoned.

Hopes of closer monetary integration were not, however, abandoned. In 1979, the **European Monetary System** came into being. The main element of this was the **exchange rate mechanism**, or ERM. The ERM was a mechanism for ensuring currency stability in Europe, with currencies allowed to fluctuate only modestly – by 2.25 per cent or 6 per cent – on either side of a central rate, determined in terms of the **European Currency Unit** (the ecu), the 'basket' currency of the the~ Britain did not join at the outset, although the other eight m~

The ERM had a mixed record. In its first eight ye~ significant currency realignments, and the aim ~f a zone of monetary stability could not be s~·

Britain, the ERM and 'Black Wednesday'

Britain finally joined the ERM in October 1990. The pound sterling was allowed a 6 per cent margin of fluctuation around a central rate against the ecu, or a rate of 2.95 German marks (deutsch marks).

Entry into the ERM was seen as stabilizing the pound on a permanent basis. John Major, chancellor of the exchequer at the time of entry and prime minister shortly afterwards, said membership of the ERM meant 'the soft option, the devaluer's option' would be no more. It was also a means of reducing Britain's then high interest rates to European levels. Interest rates were reduced from 15 per cent to 14 per cent on entry, and progressively reduced to 10 per cent in succeeding months.

Britain, however, was entering a serious recession at the time of entry and, far from providing the means of escaping it, the ERM was seen to be locking Britain into too high an exchange rate and interest rates. Less than two years later, on 'Black Wednesday', 16 September 1992, the strains grew too much and Britain was forced out of the ERM by a massive wave of selling of the pound. Once outside the ERM, the government reduced interest rates sharply, to 6 per cent, and set in train the policies that were eventually to lead to Bank of England independence. Figure 25, sterling's average value against other

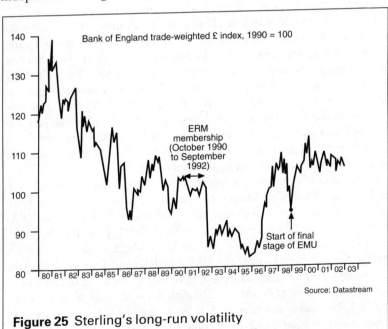

Figure 25 Sterling's long-run volatility

currencies in index terms, shows how the pound fluctuated before and after membership of the ERM.

The episode coloured British attitudes to European economic and monetary union. It also nearly precipitated the collapse of the ERM. Italy dropped out at the same time as Britain. The following summer, in July/August 1993, the ERM came under intense pressure following heavy selling of the French franc. Only by adopting a very wide currency exchange band (15 per cent) was the crisis averted. Had the ERM collapsed, it is likely the drive towards a single currency would have been halted.

Achieving EMU

The EU's second big drive towards EMU came after the signing of the Single European Act in 1986. The preamble to the Act included a restatement of the goal of achieving EMU.

Following this, a committee of central bankers and experts, under the chairmanship of Jacques Delors, the then president of the European Commission, investigated the practicalities of EMU. The **Delors report** was published in 1989.

Two years later, at Maastricht in the Netherlands, a timetable for EMU was agreed, with all member countries except Britain and Denmark agreeing to participate. (At that time Austria, Finland and Sweden were not part of the EU; they joined in 1995.) Britain and Denmark have EMU 'opt-outs' – or rather the right to opt in to EMU at a time of their choosing.

The Maastricht timetable was set as follows:

- *Stage 1:* All participating countries were to be members of the ERM and to be observing its normal fluctuation margins prior to the start of the second stage.
- *Stage 2:* On 1 January 1994, the European Monetary Institute (the European Central Bank's forerunner) would come into being and oversee countries' preparations for EMU.
- *Stage 3:* The third and final stage, including the changeover from national notes and coins to the single currency (which acquired its name, the **euro**, in 1995), would begin on 1 January 1997 if a majority of countries were ready, or by 1 January 1999 at the latest.

As it turned out, 1 January 1999 marked the euro's start as an *electronic or commercial currency* for 11 countries – Austria, Belgium, Finland, France, Germany, Ireland, Italy, Luxembourg, the Netherlands, Portugal and Spain (Greece joined soon after, in January 2001). The changeover to the euro from national notes and coins

making it easier for businesses to plan and price. A common problem for British business has been that the pound has shifted sharply, either making it difficult for them to export (the strong pound problem) or pushing up the cost of their imported materials and components (the weak pound problem).

- The opportunities to exploit the European single market would increase. Some see national currencies as 'the final barrier to trade'. With a single currency, it is argued, Europe would be able to exploit fully the economies of scale and other advantages of a large single market, and rival the USA in economic terms.

Others see additional advantages. The absence of the devaluation weapon, it is argued, would force companies, indeed whole economies, to become more competitive. Traditional high-inflation countries in the EU, such as Italy and Spain, have seen a big advantage in EMU because it enables them, under the auspices of the European Central Bank, to achieve low, German-style inflation. Britain could benefit from this. Inflation and interest rates have tended to be lower in countries such as Germany, Austria and the Netherlands, than in Britain.

Disadvantages

There are, however, also significant potential disadvantages associated with EMU.

The main doubt concerns the problem of having a single monetary policy for the whole of a very large area. This is sometimes known as the 'one size fits all' problem.

Think of it in terms of Britain. When the economy of the south-east of England is booming but the rest of the country is struggling, the onus is on the Bank of England to raise interest rates to head off inflationary pressures in the south-east, even if this would further depress other parts of the country. It would be better, but impossible, if different rates of interest were available for different regions. In EMU, this problem is writ large. Can the same interest rate be suited to conditions across 12 different countries, without causing severe problems?

One reason why the difficulty could arise is that different countries are insufficiently 'converged'. The Maastricht criteria ensured financial and fiscal convergence but not *real* economic convergence (measured by unemployment rates and, for example, whether different member states are at similar stages in the economic cycle).

In 1961 an economist called Robert Mundell wrote a paper on the subject of **optimum currency areas**. He argued that three things were needed for an optimum currency area:

- Workers had to be prepared and able to move between regions/countries in response to high unemployment where they were living and job opportunities elsewhere. They had to be 'geographically mobile'.
- Wages had to be flexible – falling wages in high unemployment areas encouraging companies within the currency area to locate there.
- There had to be scope for sufficient 'fiscal transfers' – that is by means of taxation and public spending – between parts of the currency area to offset problems.

The USA satisfies these conditions, and can be said to be an optimum currency area. Europe does not at present, although advocates of EMU would say these conditions could develop over time.

Britain and the euro

In October 1997, the Labour government announced that it was in favour in principle of joining the euro but that it would not do so in the 'first wave' in January 1999. A decision to join, it said, would be a three-way decision – supported by government, parliament and the public, in a referendum. No decision would be taken, it said, until the following parliament.

To join EMU, Britain would necessarily have to meet the five Maastricht criteria. In addition, the Chancellor set out five specifically British 'economic tests'. These were:

- Would joining EMU create better conditions for firms making long-term decisions to invest in the UK?
- How would adopting the single currency affect our financial services?
- Are business cycles and economic structures compatible so that we and others in Europe could live comfortably with euro interest rates on a permanent basis?
- If problems do emerge, is there sufficient flexibility to deal with them?
- Will joining EMU help to promote higher growth, stability and a lasting increase in jobs?

Of these, most economists believe that the third condition, convergence of economic cycles and business structures, is the most important and will be the most difficult to achieve on a genuine basis. the UK economy has traditionally been more interest-rate sensitive (because of a higher proportion of variable rate debt, notably mortgages). On June 9th 2003, the Treasury concluded that Britain was not yet ready to join the euro.

Brown stalling on euro move

By Toby Helm

Treasury officials are being held back from completing their assessment on Britain's entry to the euro because Tony Blair and Gordon Brown have not met to decide what the conclusions should be.

Sources at the Treasury admit the decision about if and when to call a referendum will depend on a 'political' judgment yet to be reached by them rather than the Treasury's much-vaunted assessment.

'The work cannot be finished until those involved in writing the conclusions know in which direction they should go,' said a senior insider. 'That depends on a meeting between the Prime Minister and Chancellor taking place.' The Treasury is compiling 18 separate reports in an assessment of whether Britain should replace the pound with the euro.

Ministers say the studies will allow a final judgment to be made on whether Mr Brown's five economic tests have been passed.

The five tests cover whether the euro would be good for investment, growth, jobs and the City and whether European and British business cycles are compatible. The Government has promised to give its decision on a referendum by June 7.

Mr Brown said yesterday the 18 studies would include reports on the exchange rate and macro-economic adjustments, the transition to the euro, an analysis of the 'framework' in which the five test analysis is being conducted and a report bringing together 'specially commissioned' papers by international academics on Britain and the euro.

Treasury officials said Mr Brown was not announcing new reports but merely the subject matter of four of the studies.

Downing Street officials suggest that Mr Blair still wants to hold a referendum next year and believes the economic tests have been met but Mr Brown is said to be far more sceptical.

On Monday, the Treasury will publish a progress report on economic reform in Europe, which will include work on how euro-zone countries are reforming their over-regulated labour markets.

In an economic debate in the Commons David Laws, the Liberal Democrat Treasury spokesman, asked Mr Brown what a negative verdict on the five tests would mean to the chances of joining the euro. 'If the assessment shows that Britain has not met the five economic tests, will that rule out a referendum on the euro for the rest of this Parliament?'

Mr Brown said he would not prejudge the assessment.

A spokesman for the anti-euro No campaign said last night: 'It's good that the Treasury is doing the detailed work on the Euro. If they take the assessment of the five tests seriously they will have to conclude they are not met.'

'With 4.6 million people unemployed in Germany, it's going to be hard to say the case for the euro is "clear and unambiguous",' added the anti-euro spokesman.

The Daily Telegraph, 13 February 2003

The Treasury emphasized all along that the assessment of the five economic tests had to be very thorough. As part of it, the Chancellor of the Exchequer published 18 separate studies, ranging from the performance of the housing market in Britain relative to other countries, to the effect on prices in the existing member countries of the changeover to euro notes and coins in January 2002. Ed Balls, the government's Chief Economic Adviser, gave a speech in 2002 setting out how previous governments had made mistakes on exchange rate policy – including the return to the Gold Standard in 1925 and membership of the ERM in 1990 – because they had not made proper economic assessments. The speech, along with other material on the euro assessment, is available on the Treasury website (www.hm-treasury.gov.uk).

The battle over euro entry, whenever it occurs, promises to be a fascinating one:

- Many (but not all) larger businesses continue to favour entry because of the savings in transaction costs, and because it will make it easier for them to do business in Europe with a single currency – and therefore no exchange rate risk (although that risk will remain outside Europe).
- Smaller businesses are, in general, more sceptical. Many do not have transaction costs with Europe.
- Public opinion is divided but on balance hostile, for both economic and political reasons.

KEY WORDS

European Union
European Coal and Steel
    Community
Treaty of Rome
European Economic
    Community
European Free Trade
    Association
Common Agricultural Policy
Common external tariff
Customs union
Single European Act
Single market
Common market
Treaty on European Union

European economic and
    monetary union
Social protocol
Trade creation
Trade diversion
Second-best solution
Werner committee
Bretton Woods
European Monetary System
Exchange rate mechanism
European Currency Unit
Delors report
Euro
Maastricht criteria
Transaction costs
Optimum currency areas

Further reading

Hill, B., Chapters 6 and 7 in *The European Union*, 4th edn., Heinemann Educational, 2001.

Russell, M., and Heathfield, D., Chapter 10 in *Inflation and UK Monetary Policy*, 3rd edn., Heinemann Educational, 1999.

Smith, D., *Will Europe Work?*, Social Market Foundation/Profile Books, 1999.

Smith, D., Chapter 13 in *Free Lunch*, Profile Books, 2003.

Useful websites

European Central Bank: www.ecb.int

European Commission: //europa.eu.int

Essay topics

1. (a) Explain the trade creation and trade diversion effects the UK has experienced as a result of joining the EU. [10 marks]

    (b) Discuss whether the UK should remain in the EU. [15 marks]

2. (a) Examine two ways in which joining a monetary union imposes constraints on the government's macroeconomic policy options. [40 marks]

    (b) Examine the benefits to a country of being a member of a monetary union. [60 marks]

    [AQA. Q1, Unit 6, Specimen Paper, 2000]

Data response question

Unilever's preparation for EMU

By January 1999, 11 European countries will have entered into a monetary union. Few companies will be as prepared for its arrival as Unilever, the Anglo-Dutch consumer group which operates in every country in the single currency zone and which makes products as diverse as ice cream, tea, margarine, Calvin Klein fragrances, Elizabeth Arden cosmetics and Persil soap powder.

The significance of the euro lies not so much in the creation of a single currency as in the contribution it will make to a much bigger process — the completion of the European Union's single market.

By removing one uncertainty in doing business across borders inside the single currency zone, the euro will allow groups such as Unilever to develop further on a European scale.

The savings from the single currency, however, will be surprisingly modest for large companies such as Unilever. Jan Naars, Unilever's

117

group treasurer, estimates the reduction in transaction costs at no more (15)
than £20 million a year — on European turnover last year of £13.6 billion.
'The benefit will be much greater for smaller companies for whom the
transaction costs are higher in proportion to sales,' he says. 'We already
operate in more than 100 countries and will still have to deal with almost
as many currencies.' (20)

Unilever will start pricing in euros for transactions between its
European subsidiaries from 1 January 1999 and for internal reporting
from 1 January 12000, but will not make an early move towards EU-wide
prices for consumers. Hans Eggerstedt, Unilever's German finance
director, expects the euro to increase the pressure for price (25)
harmonisation — it will be easier for consumers to spot the variations
inside the monetary union. However, large organizations like Unilever
are already comparing prices and buying supplies on an EU-wide scale.

The single currency will also affect the allocation of resources within the
single market. 'The UK will be an unpredictable currency area for the rest (30)
of Europe,' says Mr Eggerstedt, 'despite its advantages as a
manufacturing centre. We already have to deal with the consumer, the
competition and the authorities — so we like to eliminate other
uncertainties.'

'One more step to the single market', *The Financial Times*, 4 June 1998 (adapted)

(a) Briefly explain what is meant by the following terms:
    (i) monetary union (line 2) [2 marks]
    (ii) the single market (line 9). [2 marks]
(b) State and explain **one** way in which the euro is significant for 'the
    completion of the European Union's single market' (line 9).
    [2 marks]
(c) (i) What is meant by 'transaction costs' (line 15)? [1 mark]
    (ii) Why are the benefits of reduction costs 'greater for smaller
        companies' (line 17)? [2 marks]
    (iii) Explain **another** reason why some companies may benefit more
        than others from the European single currency. [2 marks]
(d) 'The UK will be an unpredictable currency area for the rest of Europe,
    despite its advantages as a manufacturing centre' (lines 30–31).
    (i) Explain why the UK might have 'advantages as a
        manufacturing centre'. [3 marks]
    (ii) To what extent might the UK economy be disadvantaged by
        the decision to delay entry into Economic and Monetary
        Union? [6 marks]
    [OCR, Q1, Paper 4385, March 2000]

Conclusion

This book has tried, as in the earlier editions, to bring out the multi-faceted nature of economic policy in the UK. Economic policy under 'New' Labour can be characterized along the following lines. Macroeconomic policy (monetary and fiscal policy) has been aimed at producing economic stability – no return to boom and bust – while directing more resources into public services. Microeconomic policy has had two main aims. The first is to increase employment by making it easier for people to take up work, for example through the New Deal and tax credits. The second has been to increase productivity, by encouraging firms to invest and by promoting greater competition.

There are three things to emphasize. One is that the policy emphasis does change over time. In the 1970s and 80s, such was the concern over inflation, even hyper-inflation, that other economic goals, notably full employment, appeared to be relegated. Maintaining sound finances became the priority. But sound finances, while necessary, can never be the sole aim of economic policy. Achieving the highest possible level of employment, and the fastest sustainable increase in living standards, are ultimately what it is all about.

The second point is that a book of this size can never be comprehensive. Mention of the word sustainable in the preceding paragraph reminds me that there is little in this book about the use of economic instruments, such as taxation, for environmental purposes. That may be an issue which rises in importance over the next few years.

Finally, as noted in the introduction, economics is a living, evolving subject, and this is particularly the case for economic policy. Change makes it a challenging subject to teach, and to keep abreast of, but it also makes it all the more rewarding. Policy evolves, but sometimes it comes around in circles. Knowing what is new, and what is recycled, is part of the fun. The interaction of politics and economics, which is the essence of economic policy, is fascinating, and deserves the widest possible audience. Newspaper articles, including my own, are one source of information and analysis. I am also happy to enter into dialogue (e-mail: david.smith@sunday-times.co.uk), although neither I nor your teachers would want me to be answering your essay questions!

In a wider sense, economic policy and its consequences are all around us. Everybody should have a basic grounding in how the process works. This is what I tried to do in my recent book *Free Lunch*, and it is what I have tried to do again in this edition of *UK Current Economic Policy*.

Index